At Work and Play

At Work and Play

Biblical Insight for Daily Obedience

Bradshaw Frey
William Ingram
Thomas E. McWhertor
William David Romanowski

PAIDEIA PRESS
Jordan Station, Ontario, Canada

Canadian Cataloguing in Publication Data

Main entry under title:
At work and play : Biblical insight for daily obedience

Bibliography: p.
ISBN 0-88815-154-3

1. Christian life – Biblical teaching. 2. College students – Conduct of
life. 3. College students – Religious life. I. Frey, Bradshaw.

BV4531.2.A8 1986   248.8'34   C86-093396-2

The Scripture quotations in this publication are from the New International Version, copyright © 1978 by the New York International
Bible Society.

Cover design by Bonnie LaVallee.

ISBN 0-88815-154-3
Printed in Canada.

Contents

Foreword

The Christian student entering the halls of academia will find that the Christian faith is not so much challenged as it is ignored. The Judeo-Christian belief system is not rejected; it is treated as a remnant of an earlier era no longer capable of surviving the flood of secular intellectual insights which have inundated "sophisticated" thinkers since the Enlightenment. The academic community generally does not reject Yahweh, but instead, in the words of George Santayana, "bids Him a fond farewell."

The responsibility of the Christian intellectual is to integrate faith and knowledge. The data, insights, facts and discoveries of those in academia must not be dealt with as though they belonged to a world other than that in which faith exists. Those who speak the language of the liberal arts and sciences must not be left to live in a world devoid of a Christian witness because there are none who can speak their language or demonstrate how their knowledge points beyond itself to God revealed in Scripture.

The tasks of the Christian entering the modern day halls of learning are threefold. First of all it is essential to grow in spiritual maturity and to gain a deeper understanding of the Bible. This task will have to be accomplished outside the context of the formal academic program. Private Bible study and discussions with fellow Christians are an essential part of this process.

The availability of time for such religious exercises will be limited and often the pressures and demands of academic assignments will threaten to crowd them out of the student's busy schedule. However, neglect of these disciplines will prove spiritually disastrous. Without a regular diet of biblical truth and without a Christian fellowship group to maintain what Peter Berger calls "a plausibility structure" for these truths, the student's Christian convictions may gradually dissipate. Like Samson when he was shorn through the treachery of Delilah, the student may wake one day not knowing that the spirit has departed from him/her.

On the other hand, forming a support group with Christian colleagues can provide an instrument for the maintenance of faithfulness and an impetus for spiritual growth. John Wesley, the founder of Methodism, established such a support group while studying at Oxford. That group met regularly each morning for prayer and Bible study. So methodically did this support group gather for mutual encouragement and correction that they earned the nickname "methodists" among the Oxford dons. However, history attests to the fact that it was this "holy club" (as its members called it) that enabled these young Christians not only to hold on to their beliefs, but challenged them to develop a Christian world view which later changed the consciousness of England. It would be well for contemporary Christian students to learn from the Wesleyan example.

Secondly, the Christian is obligated to learn *all* that is being taught in the books assigned and the lectures attended. There is no excuse for wasting the precious opportunity to "study to show yourself approved unto God, a workman that needs not to be ashamed, rightly dividing the word of truth" (II Tim. 2:15). Just as Paul adroitly used the teachings of the ancient Greek philosophers and poets to lead Athenians to Christ, so the Christian must be equipped to use the theories and propositions of secularists to further the course of Christ's Kingdom.

Even ideas which stand in diametrical opposition to Christian doctrine should be understood. The evangelical student must know those things which must be challenged if a solid stand for truth is to be made. The shortcomings of philosophies and theories which deny the validity of Christianity must be explored and exposed. The Christian student must learn to answer the arguments of secular intellectuals and, in the words of Scripture, ". . . Always be prepared to make a defense to any one who calls you to account for the hope that is in you . . ." (I Peter 3:15). A liberal arts education is a privilege of a select few. Those few are expected to be apologists for the rest of us and this requires that we know what our challengers propose.

This book will provide a good starting place. In chapter after chapter, Christian scholars endeavor to prepare the collegian for the anti-Christian arguments and perspectives rampant in their respective disciplines. An annotated bibliography will provide source material for students who need help in developing an antithetical approach to secularized orientations in various academic fields. Use this material well. Your survival as a Christian intellectual might depend upon it.

Thirdly, the Christian student should learn to integrate belief systems with the valid data and discoveries of the academic community. More times than not what is learned will enhance the world view of the Christian rather than threaten it. The students, if properly prepared, will find that even the theories and insights of atheistic and agnostic academicians can enhance one's understanding of Christian truth and give a fuller understanding of the nature of God's social and physical worlds. Truth is truth, regardless of who discovers it and, whenever truth is discovered, it points beyond itself to God. I wrote a book entitled, *Partly Right*, in order to show that some of Christianity's most notorious enemies (ie. Sigmund Freud, Karl Marx and Friedrich Nietzsche) declared some things that are not only true, but important for Christians to learn. Truth, even when discovered by those opposed to our biblical faith, can be integrated into a Christian world view and become part of the apology for our theology. Once again, this book will prove useful. The authors do not look with disparagement upon the findings of secular scholars; on the contrary, they respectfully show the strengths and weaknesses of their formulations.

This book is not an exhaustive handbook which will answer every question posed by the secular intellectual community, but it will serve as a model to show students how to address the task of integrating the truths of the college classroom with the truths of the Bible. It is an unusual book, and in it the reader will discover an important source of help in finding a path through the maze called "a college education."

I must offer one last warning. In some cases the student may find that reconciliation between the truths of secular scholarship and the truths of the Scripture proves impossible. In such cases, I suggest that the Christian student "bracket"

the discoveries of academia and hold fast to the Word of God.
Time and time again the "truth" of the proud intellectuals is
displaced by new discoveries. But the truth of God abides
forever. The authors of this book are committed to that
abiding truth and make a notable effort to show the fledgling
intellectual how to stand fast in that faith.

December, 1985   Dr. Anthony Campolo,
                      Chairperson of the Department of Sociology
                            at Eastern College, St. Davids, PA

Preface

As our society races at breakneck speed after the idol of technological progress, our learning and institutions of learning suffer. Learning is reduced to technique or method cut off from its philosophical and historical roots. In our extensive work with college and university students, we have been alarmed to see that the basic movements in the history of thought and their accompanying influences are ignored as students pursue the easiest or most widely accepted method.

In *All of Life Redeemed*, we elaborated a Christian foundation or world view with which a person could approach contemporary society. At that point, we were unable even to approach specific disciplines. In this present volume, we hope to help Christians begin to ground their knowledge of these disciplines in a biblical context. These brief chapters are not critiques of the various disciplines but are rather attempts to dialogue with perspectives taken in those various fields from our Christian perspective.

In each chapter, after an introductory chapter on being a Christian student, we put a particular discipline in a historical context, examine major trends in the field, raise questions from a Christian perspective and offer some new direction. We hope that raising these basic and introductory issues will encourage students and others to investigate more deeply their fields and not put their Christianity aside as they do.

Finally, three of the authors are indebted to Thomas E. McWhertor for his general supervision of the project and his tireless efforts to bring this manuscript together.

May God be glorified in our efforts!

Dedication

This book is published in memory of Dr. Peter J. Steen and in honor of Dr. Bernard Zylstra. They have glorified Christ in their lives and inspired us to live as citizens of the Kingdom of God. May God bless our efforts in this volume as He has blessed the lives of countless men and women through these men, His servants.

About the Authors

The authors of this material are involved in the ministry of the Coalition for Christian Outreach, a cooperative effort of colleges, universities and churches to reach students for Christ. All were coauthors of *All of Life Redeemed* as well.

Bradshaw L. Frey

Brad serves with the Coalition as Assistant Dean of Religious Services at Geneva College in Beaver Falls, PA. He is a graduate of Geneva College and holds an M.Div. and S.T.M. from Pittsburgh Theological Seminary. He is currently a Ph.D. candidate in the Foundations of Education at the University of Pittsburgh. Brad has published articles on a variety of topics in numerous magazines, including *Decision* and *The Presbyterian Journal*.

William E. Ingram

Bill serves as Specialist for Management Services in the administrative offices of the Coalition. He is a graduate of the University of Maryland and holds an M.Div. from Wesley Theological Seminary. He is presently pursuing work in adult education, planning to apply that work within the context of the local congregation. Bill is a member of the Associate Reformed Presbyterian Church.

Thomas E. McWhertor

Tom is Director of Communications, Resource Development and the JUBILEE Conference for the Coalition and in this capacity serves as coordinator of this project. He is a graduate of Grove City College and holds an M.Div. from Gordon-Conwell Theological Seminary. He presently serves on the national board of directors of the Association for Public Justice, a Christian citizen's group seeking to nurture responsible, active citizenship in accord with Christian political principles.

William David Romanowski

Bill is a professional musician and a Resource Specialist with the Coalition. He is a graduate of Indiana University of Pennsylvania and holds an M.A. from Youngstown State University. He is also an adjunct instructor at Geneva College and Calvin College. Bill is the author of articles in popular publications such as *Contemporary Christian Magazine* and is presently working on a book dealing with the interrelationship between the popular arts and popular culture since World War II. As a musician and performer, Bill tours widely with two shows: "William David Romanowski in Concert" and "Let 'em Build Their Kingdom . . . A Penetrating Analysis of Popular Music and Culture."

Acknowledgments

A book like this is never the product of one person or small group of people. There are countless people who should rightly be acknowledged for their contribution to this effort.

Four friends stand out for their contributions in the form of original material for four of the chapters included here: Peggy Berns Mindrebo wrote the original material for the arts chapter, Howie Shultz wrote the original material on sports, Terry Thomas wrote the material for the education chapter, and Christy Wauzzinski contributed the original material for the psychology chapter. It is not exaggeration to say that the insights and strengths of those chapters are theirs. As we edited and rewrote to fit our present format, we surely bear the blame for any shortcomings—not these original contributors.

We would also like to thank quite a number of people who must go unnamed for their interaction and evaluation of individual chapters throughout the writing process. There were times when we wondered whether we were on track or not and these saints encouraged us and redirected us with their critical (and crucial) evaluations.

Cathie Sunderman deserves heartfelt thanks for her patience in typing and constant editing work to help the manuscript keep up with our changes and our editor at Paideia Press, Patricia Weaver, deserves much thanks for making our work more understandable here and in *All of Life Redeemed*, our earlier publication.

Our families deserve much credit for the inspiration and motivation which they have provided us. Sue, Scott and Andrew; Jeanette, Amy and Charlie; Janice, Kata, Annie, Christopher and Colin; and Donna and Michael have put up with much from somewhat driven and eccentric husbands and fathers. Our prayer is that our children will benefit from these pages in time and stand firmly on our shoulders to be salt and light in the world.

We would like to thank countless men and women who have been involved in the ministry of the Coalition for Christian Outreach. Whether they be founders, board members, supporters, former or present staff, or former or present students—all have contributed to making the message of redemption in Christ clear in our day and in that sense contributed to this effort. A special thanks must be given to Robert R. Long, Executive Director of the Coalition for Christian Outreach, for his leadership and unceasing efforts in our cause of reaching the leaders of tomorrow who study on the campuses today.

Finally, it is very fitting that this book is released just in time to commemorate the 10th annual JUBILEE Conference— JUBILEE 1986. The JUBILEE Conference and the ideas it embodies are the fire in which this book was forged. Speakers over the past ten years should easily see their contributions on these pages.

May God be honored with our efforts.

December, 1985   6740 Fifth Avenue
                                          Pittsburgh, PA 15208 USA

Chapter 1

The Christian Student Today

"Cop-out!"
"Sell-out!"
"Drop-out!"
"Burn-out!"

What happens to a Christian when he or she becomes a student at a college or university?

Some "cop-out." These Christians see no relationship or connection between their Christian faith and their studies. Faith in Christ, for these Christians, dictates certain extra-curricular involvements (prayer partners, Bible studies, fellowship meetings and personal evangelism), but not any particular differences in the way they study or in the way they write papers. These Christians tend to isolate their faith in the "personal" areas of life and often isolate themselves from the mainstream of campus (and cultural) life.

Those who "sell-out" do see the need to relate their faith in Christ to the exigencies of everyday living. However, without proper grounding, they tend to accommodate their Christian faith to the challenges of the academic world. These believers intertwine Christian beliefs and non-Christian beliefs so as to gain academic respectability, but in the process lose the essence of the Christian faith which should lie at the heart of their activities.

The "drop-outs" are those who have seen the inconsistency of the "sell-out" or "cop-out" options and have rejected the Christian faith altogether. These people have been unable to sustain their faith against the onslaught of academic attack or in the quagmire of inconsistency. They have chosen to trust some alternative to the Gospel. Sometimes well-meaning but ill-informed Christians who have "sold-out" or "copped-out" drive these people away; nevertheless, they choose to reject faith in Christ, or "drop-out."

Those who "burn-out" are Christians who strive to build their studies upon a Christian foundation appropriately, yet get bogged down. Sensing the integrality of faith in Christ, these Christians struggle to relate academic work to their Christian faith, but there is too much work for too few to do and the few get tired and give up the work.[1]

The risk the Christian takes in the university is great. The odds of even a single student avoiding all of the pitfalls are slim. Is it any wonder that Christianity is not on the cutting edge of our modern culture? If it is true that the leaders of our world tomorrow are on our campuses today, we need to develop a generation of Christian students who will make an impact for Christ in our world.

A Christian student is one whom God has called to the office of "student" for a time. A Christian student bases both life and studies on the confession that Christ is Lord and the view of life that follows from that confession. A Christian student studies twice—both to learn what the world says about the subject being studied and to learn and develop his or her own views from a Christian basis.

The Calling of a Christian Student

It seems that there is confusion in our day regarding even as basic an issue as the task of a student who is a Christian. Many will argue persuasively that the role of the Christian student is that of an "evangelist" within the college or university context. Those holding this view charge the Christian who takes the role of student with the responsibility of proclaiming the salvation of Christ in the non-Christian setting. Like the missionary in a foreign country, the student must lead those in the university to an understanding of the Christ of Scripture.

In fact, this seems to be the dominant view of what it means to be a Christian student in our day. Students are taught how to do "personal evangelism" before they are taught how to study. Many Christians deem it more important to attend the Bible study or fellowship meeting than to attend the engineering society or study for the exam the next morning. Since the primary task is that of "evangelist," it doesn't matter if our studies and future vocations suffer, so long as we equip ourselves and obediently seek to "save souls" around us.

The opposite position maintains that the Christian student is in the university to acquire knowledge, in a sense, "apart from the faith." Those who advocate this position encourage the student to seek academic and professional pursuits apart from the fellowship of believers and with no sense of mission. This is a type of "sabbatical" from church and religious duties in order to study unhampered. The assumption is that upon completion of studies, the student will again assume Christian responsibilities and integrate them back into everyday life.

Both of these extremes, the "evangelist" and "sabbatical" understandings of what it means to be a Christian student, err in compartmentalizing the Christian faith into certain restricted areas of life. The "evangelist" sees Christian activities limited to evangelism and personal piety because he or she is unable to see how the Gospel implies action for everyday life. The "sabbatical" advocates think that issues of faith can easily be set aside while other pursuits in life go on. Neither extreme recognizes the root nature of faith, the way that Christian belief lies at the foundation of all of life and cannot be identified with particular activities or removed from others. True faith demands that it direct our thinking and our living on every level. To limit the student to being an "evangelist" ignores myriad activities and areas which are under the Lordship of Christ as well. To consider setting aside Christian responsibilities for a season of study, contradicts the reason a Christian studies. Certainly the Christian student must learn what it means to be a student in a Christian way.

There is another set of contrasting misconceptions about what it means to be a Christian student. Many deny that "student" is a calling at all; rather, the role of student, they say, is merely a phase of development, another stop along the way to one's real calling. In this view, students are "in limbo," awaiting a calling or preparing for a calling in the future somewhere.

On the other hand, others maintain that the calling of student is reserved for a few with whom God has endowed special gifts of insight and study capacities. They spend their lives in study and research, and have little in common with the thousands who populate college and university campuses today. Real students, those whom God has called to be students, will be students for a lifetime—so these interpreters think.

These extremes, "no calling" and "select few," miss the organic nature of our calling by God. To say that there is no calling of "student" because the task is not permanent, implies that God cannot call individuals or groups to particular tasks at one time and other tasks at another time. To advocate that our calling is unchangeable denies that we can change professions without repentance and forgiveness. Indeed, God has and will continue to call men and women to various tasks at various times in their lives.

To limit the role of student to a developmental phase fails to grasp the volitional nature of being a student and the responsibilities which accompany it. We need not be life-long "students" to be called to study to present ourselves approved of God in whatever area we pursue. Every Christian, from child to senior citizen, is called by God to pursue his or her vocation in a way that honors the God who created him or her. The child is called to be a child, responsive to parental instruction and supervision. The student is called to learn, and the adult is called to live out his faith or her faith in whatever ways God has gifted or prepared him or her.[2]

The Christian student is called by God to explore, understand and master knowledge about the Creator, His creation, and His norms for living. Just as all Christians must proclaim that Lord they serve in their lives and vocations, so the Christian student must study as unto the Lord. It is not a certain field of study or vocational goal that makes one a Christian student. Rather, it is the way a student makes basic decisions, the assumptions upon which those decisions are built, and the way he or she uses that learning in the ongoing task of properly developing the potential of God's creation.

The Christian student who is preparing for a future profession is charged with the same responsibility now to prepare Christianly as he or she will be charged with the responsibility of professional work. If God has called some to be students, if only for a while, that means that those Christian students are to study in a Christian way just as those whom God has called to be artists, business people, engineers, or preachers must work in a Christian way. Neither the professional nor the student can "baptize" his or her work with a little prayer and evangelism and expect that to be the end of it. Rather, Christian students and professionals (as well as laborers and homemakers) must seek to reflect the Lord whom they serve in their work. That means for the Christian student that subjects studied, study habits, the assumptions behind what is learned, how the information is derived and finally how it is applied—all of these must reflect the Lordship of Christ. Likewise, the professional must work out the service performed, the way it is performed, the quality of the work, the assumptions upon which work methods are based and the structure of the organization—all from a basis of how Christ is most honored in this work.

The Christian student's first motivation is a desire to honor God with all of his or her life. By contrast, most students today are committed to learning technical skills as quickly as possible to enable themselves to get the best possible job. The best job is one which provides "the good life"; the affluence to escape from life and work into dreams, retirement plans, and leisure activity. The Christian student must stand out in contrast.

While most students today are "looking out for number one," Christian students ought to be building a foundation for service to God and neighbor. While students today are motivated by a desire for material success, Christian students should live knowing there is more to life. While students today are enticed by advertising, popular culture, and our educational system into working for the sake of material benefits, Christian students must resist this temptation, and endeavor to work for the sake of the Kingdom of God.

Three such students are Dave, Paul and Kim. Dave is finishing medical school. He has struggled for three years with his school's attempt to mold him into a "professional." He is planning his internship for an inner-city hospital, for he has learned that medical care in our society is concentrated on middle and upper middle class suburbanites. He is interning in the inner city because he believes that he must bring the healing to the people who need it most, to the inner city (or to rural areas as well).

Paul recently graduated from law school. He now works as a lawyer for a congressional committee. Though advised not to come to Washington, D.C., he believed that the renewing presence of Christians with a strong sense of justice is critical for the future of our nation. Though his counsel is often refused, still he attempts to speak a clear word of justice within the structure of government.

Kim has both a deep concern about racism and a husband with a background in construction. Their hope is to start their own contracting company which will renovate housing for the underprivileged and give young people marketable skills for future jobs. All three of these students have used their schooling as foundations for the work they will do as Kingdom citizens.

Christian students must demonstrate a healthy view of life and vocation in the way they live their lives, aware of the reality of sin and its self-centeredness. They must examine their motives and those of their classmates and professors. As students they are responsible to God, to their fellow Christians, to their fellow students and to the world in which they live. Christian students must appropriate gifts and abilities God has given and use those gifts in the classroom, study hall and residence hall in ways which honor God and demonstrate love and concern for their neighbors.

Once again we emphasize that the vocation of student is Christian not because of the field studied or the occupation sought or the witness accomplished. Rather, it is Christian because of how decisions are made and how work is done in particular situations. The work of a Christian student should prepare and assist young men and women to serve, to care, to show mercy and to express themselves creatively with grace.

A Christian student's work is based on the sovereignty of God the Creator and Sustainer of all things and on the understanding that humanity is that part of the creation which reflects the Creator. These realities form the foundation for a certain way of observing life. This way of observation is "pre-scientific" in that it determines the way to further observe and evaluate reality. This special pre-theoretic foundation separates the Christian student from all others when it is built upon consistently. For this reason, we must understand it thoroughly.

The Christian Reality

"In the beginning God created the heavens and the earth . . ." (Gen 1:1). "For by him all things were created: things in heaven and on earth, visible and invisible, . . . all things were created by him and for him. He is before all things, and in him all things hold together" (Col. 1:15-17). The scriptural message is clear throughout: the triune God is the Creator and Sustainer of all things. This is the most basic of assumptions for all Christians; foundational, too, for the Christian student. This world that is the object of inquiry, study and mastery is not a human creation, to be manipulated however human beings desire. Rather, the potentialities, boundaries and timing are established by God: Father, Son and Holy Spirit. Humans are merely creatures, created by God to most clearly reflect His own image within the creation, and to do so by developing the potentialities of the creation that He has established.

Yet the emphasis of the biblical narrative is not on humanity's success in carrying out the Creator's design, but rather on our miserable failure and need for redemption, time and time again. All people are created in the image of God, but history has shown that people have repeatedly rebelled, choosing to assert their own autonomy rather than reflect the image of the Creator. This assertion of autonomy, or selfishness, was at the root of the fall into sin; but fallen humanity still receives (not seeking it) redemption by the Sovereign God—through the life, death, resurrection and ascension of Christ, the God-man. Such redemption is the basis for Christian living, best described as obedient service to God in gratitude for His grace.[3]

The fact that the triune God is the Creator of all things has tremendous implications for our task as students. We are not creating or inventing, in any ultimate sense; instead Christian students know that they are discovering the potential within the good creation of God and discovering ways in which that potential can be cultivated to enhance the creation. However, students not only discover and employ potentialities, they also examine the structures as God created them, seeking the norms that are inherent in the creation as a guide to the task of rebuilding a fallen world.

Those who lack this Christian foundation see no normativity in creation and lodge potentiality in humanity itself. They believe that whatever humanity can do is right and that the only limits should be the time it takes for skills and capacities to evolve. The notion that humans are the creators par excellence ignores created order and structure.

Humanity created in the image of God is a concept foreign to contemporary times. The view of humanity which permeates our world today sees the human race as the measure of all things. If a man or woman cannot do something (in a verifiable, scientifically repeatable way), then it cannot be done. If humanity, through scientific inquiry, cannot demonstrate that something exists, it doesn't exist. The contemporary view not only puts humanity at the top of the

evolutionary ladder, it assumes that humanity itself has
created the ladder and is that by which all else is judged: quite
a different starting point than God as Creator and
man/woman as image bearer of God, created to serve Him.

"Newspeak," "Double think," and "Double study!"

In Orwell's *1984*, "newspeak" was commonly employed
by the bureaucracy to say one thing and mean another.
"Newspeak" was used to bring the actions of the people into
line with the aims and directions decided by the leaders of the
society which Orwell pictured. Certainly the "double think"
that Orwell envisioned was despicable because it
manipulated people in a way that was almost beyond their
ability to resist. People had to hear one thing but interpret it
in an opposite way.

There is a sense in which the Christian student in the
modern college or university finds himself or herself in a
similar situation. Faith commitments have been couched in
scientific jargon to make them credible. "Newspeak" calls
one perspective neutral or academically credible, and all the
others biased, naive, or superstitious. Nothing could be further from the truth. Yet this "newspeak" has been commonly
accepted.

The result of such rampant "newspeak" has been equally
rampant "double think," particularly among Christians and
other so-called "biased groups." "Double think" occurs when
we have been persuaded to believe that one perspective (bias)
is academically acceptable, and yet maintain another "personal" faith (bias). Then we need to think on two levels. On one
level we think just like everybody else, looking at life and living from the perspective of those assumptions. Simultaneously, we reserve the private areas of life for quite another faith
commitment (bias) and so "double think" our way through
life.

Using the Christian faith as an example of a bias existing
in the midst of a non-Christian society, let me illustrate the
dilemma of "double think" as we experience it today.

The modern student is faced with an educational system
that is riddled with "newspeak" from primary through collegiate levels. In the name of academic acceptability a view of
life is taught (dare we say required) which has its own biases.
Those biases should be open to examination. In every field man
is viewed as the center of the universe, the highest source of

appeal. In every field, a certain scientific method of empirical verification (which again centers on man) determines truth from lie, myth from reality. In every field, a certain closed system is assumed to encompass all of reality with no possibility of anything coming from outside that system.

The Christian immediately faces a dilemma when entering such an educational system, for a Christian believes that God is the Creator and center of the universe, the highest source of appeal. The Christian believes in a God who is beyond empirical verification and outside any closed system of reality. Further, the Christian believes that God is personally active in the creation. "Double think" occurs precisely when Christians try to hold both views simultaneously. In the name of academic acceptability many Christians adopt the non-Christian viewpoint in public areas of life—including the educational system. Alongside these beliefs, they maintain personal or private beliefs in God who is beyond empirical verification, but not relevant to public areas. In this "double think" position, Christians maintain two opposing views of the world, one for their public (common) lives and another for their private (personal) lives. They live their lives out of two conflicting views of the world.

Such "double think" is schizophrenic. It is contradictory, and certainly is not Christian. God has created us to be whole people not torn asunder by opposing views of life and the world. Rather than "double think," we are to see a whole new formulation that differs radically from the non-Christian view of life. As opposed to the supposed "neutral" view which dominates, Christians should assert their own view of life and the world which point for point refutes the opposing views.

Instead of "double thinking," the Christian student should "double study." He or she is to develop a uniquely Christian perspective and to fashion alternatives out of this world view. However, the task of the Christian student is not finished until he or she has mastered the material from the dominant world view and then properly critiqued it in light of the uniquely Christian perspective. Those who hold a Christian world view must "double study"—to master both the truth and the lie.

Let us not be naive; "double study" is not easy. It is hard to master a view of life which is not your own without falling prey to it. But it is harder still to critique that world view in all its particulars and offer a Christian alternative in the midst of the debate. It requires dedication and time—much more time than what it takes merely to "get by." What is more, if you "double study" you will tread a path where few have gone before. There are only a few resources and those only barely scratch the surface of the field or else delve into subtleties that appear abstract or obtuse. The "average" Christian student will have to spend many hours examining the critiques and alternatives available and then sift through to reach his or her own conclusions. It will take special effort to find Christian sources and more special effort to convince Christian classmates that they must make a communal effort to achieve a Christian perspective.

"Double study" may mean that one doesn't have time for certain extracurricular activities or perhaps that course work will take an extra year or consume summers. "Double study" may mean extended and uncomfortable ongoing discussion with professors or antagonistic students or perhaps mean that guided study, reading and tutorial courses become necessary. "Double study" may mean that a student should take course work at several institutions to best balance the world views presented.

"Double think" is the "cop out" option mentioned early in this chapter. It is not a legitimate option for a Christian student. "Double study" is the singular course of action that allows the Christian student integrity. Although the task may seem overwhelming, such a person can have enormous influence. This person's heart commitment energizes his or her life as a student so that he or she brings the touch of redemption to many aspects of student life.

Portrait of a Christian as a Student

As you turn off the alarm, the agenda for the day flashes by your mind's eye: it will be the busiest day of the week. Quickly you dress and once outside gasp at the cold wind that whistles through your jogging togs this late fall day. Your run gives you plenty of time to reflect about last evening. It was an exceptional student government meeting; you don't attend many that are so good. There was a good discussion about justice in the disbursement of activity fees. How remarkable that the rights of the minority were honored and the major stumbling block passed without comment. Discussions and votes like that confirm your decision to invest time and energy in that area of student life. Just thinking about it makes the drudgery of the run easier.

Returning to your apartment, you wake your roommate as you hurry into the shower—only a few minutes until your weekly breakfast meeting. A few minutes later, you pull on the clothes carefully chosen last night. They aren't the latest fad, but are neat and clean and accent your own body well without screaming for attention. Arriving only a little late, you meet your friends coming down the hallway; together you quickly pass through the cafeteria line to find a quiet corner for yourselves. While you eat you discuss world events, happenings on campus, and the dates scheduled for the weekend. Soon you begin to talk about your own struggles as a Christian and then study together; this week it is Zechariah 14. Your time of prayer together ends, and you take a minute before your nine o'clock class to mail a postcard home and pick up your mail at the post office.

The nine o'clock class is your toughest. In fact, it is the reason that you decided to take a reduced load this term and take a summer course to catch up. Why is it that this professor doesn't allow a Christian view to be expressed openly in this class? As you do your best to answer the only question addressed to you today, you can see the displeasure on his face. Yet today he returns the research papers, and much to your surprise your mark is high, and the brief note at the end says that despite his disagreements, he can't fault your thoroughness, your consistency or your alternatives. Perhaps there is hope that you can be yourself yet.

Following class, you get together with a group of friends in the library study room to work at developing a Christian perspective in your field. Of the seven, three of you have the nine o'clock class together, two had it last year and two will take it next year. This group has been the main source of strength in the struggle to forebear and offer an alternative Christian perspective. As you compare your progress on various group projects, it is easy to see the value of such a group in your life. Without friends encouraging you in your effort to figure out a Christian view in the midst of so many contrary perspectives, you never would have known the bankruptcy of the other views or the joy of sensing the truth in adversity. The group sometimes starts with prayer, as it did today, but predictably ends with "hot and heavy" discussion and analysis.

The next class ends and after a quick lunch with several new students, you take some time to read the newspaper in the library before digging into an afternoon of study. During a

*break to the snack shop, you met two people: one you were not
looking for, the other you were hoping to see. First, as you
walked away from the soda fountain, your nine-o'clock class
professor beckoned you to sit at his table. After some small talk
about the terrible football season and the promising basketball
team, you discussed your paper at some length. The conversation was cordial, but the differences were sharp, and as the
conversation ended you were glad that you had been up to date
on all of your work and reading parallel material from a Christian perspective as well. The odds are that you will never convince him, but at least he knows why you as a Christian must
critique his approach and the ways that you think alternative-
ly.*

*Just as you were about to step back into the library, you
ran into your date for Saturday night. Since the community
play that you had planned to see received such poor reviews in
the midweek paper, you agreed instead to do some shopping
together and then get a bite to eat afterwards. Both of you
agreed to check with your respective roommates to see if they
would like to go along, with or without dates, and you returned
to your studying. That relationship is a special one and well
worth the struggles to maintain it. Your mutual love for Christ
and respect for one another make sexual conquests for the
sake of your self-esteem senseless.*

*Dinner that night is a delight, for you've been invited to
the home of a family from the church which you attend. It's
always good to get into a home since you travel to your own
home only at holidays. The sound of children playing and the
fatherly and motherly conversation is refreshing. You return
to the apartment for some more studying and some time with
your roommate. As you go up the stairs, you reflect on the
specialness of the relationship between you and your roommate. Although you are from varied families, backgrounds and
races, your friendship and encouragement for one another has
been a mainstay in each of your lives. As difficult as your
schedules sometimes are, you spend time together because it is
refreshing, insightful, and fun. This will be your best time
together this week since the schedule is so busy and your jobs
will consume most of the day on Saturday.*

*Your evening is uneventful as you visit together and make
final preparations for three big classes tomorrow. The time is
pleasantly interrupted by the couple from the apartment
upstairs who invite you both up for a snack while watching the
news. You'll need to stay up a little late to finish the extra*

reading for the eight o'clock class—so much for your run tomorrow morning.

As you retire for the night, you recognize with gratitude God's provision for your life and His grace in Christ. As you pray for specific items you remember your classes, your profs, your Christian friends, your non-Christian friends (and opportunities to again explain the Gospel to them), your studies and your family. Most of all, however, you pray that your efforts as a Christian student will be worthy of Him who has called you, that you would adequately put to use the gifts and abilities He has given you and that your efforts would be confirmed and used to further His Kingdom.

Why is it that you live the way you do? Certainly not for the grades or the future job or to impress anyone. No, you live the way you do because God so loved the world that He sent His own Son. A Christian student's goal is to please God, to make Him happy, to demonstrate the wisdom and glory of God in everything done and to demonstrate that in Christ are all the treasures of knowledge and wisdom.

Notes

1. Brian Walsh, "How to Think Your Way Through College", *HIS* Magazine, November, 1983, Vol. 44, No. 2, pp. 26-29.
2. For more on this theme, see *All of Life Redeemed: Biblical Insight for Daily Obedience*, Bradshaw L. Frey, et al, Paideia Press (Jordan Station, Ontario, Canada)—note particularly chapter 6, section one.
3. For more on this theme, see *All of Life Redeemed*; particularly note chapters 1-3.

Annotated Bibliography

Frey, Bradshaw; Ingram, William; McWhertor, Thomas E.; and Romanowski, William David, *All of Life Redeemed*, Jordan Station, Ontario, Canada: Paideia Press, Ltd., 1983.
By the authors of the present volume—obviously we highly recommend it as a primer in the basics of a biblical view of life. We heartily recommend that those interested in further developing themes of this chapter and book consult *All of Life Redeemed* and the suggestions there "for further reading."

Guinness, Os, *The Gravedigger File*, Downers Grove, IL: Inter-
Varsity Press, 1983.
     Written in the style of Lewis' *Screwtape Letters*, this
     poignant book analyzes sociological phenomena that
     have sapped the vitality from the church in the closing
     years of the twentieth century. Guinness is particularly
     adept at making the secularization of the Christian faith
     understandable in nonreligious lingo and then develops
     the themes at length. Guinness is the author of *The Dust
     of Death* (IVP) and *In Two Minds* (IVP) and was formerly
     an associate of Francis Schaeffer at L'Abri.

Hermann, Kenneth, *University Study in Christian Perspective*,
     monograph available from the Institute for Christian
     Studies, 229 College Street, Toronto, Ontario. Canada
     M5T 1R4 (416-979-2331).
     A brief argument for an integral Christian perspective
     in the life and studies of contemporary students. Her-
     mann is the director of a Christian study center for Kent
     State University, Ohio, and this paper is a great starting
     place for Christians seeking to glorify Christ in their
     lives as students.

Levine, Arthur, *When Dreams and Heros Died: A Portrait of
     Today's College Student*, Washington, DC: Jossey-Bass,
     1983.
     In this book sponsored by the Carnegie Commission on
     Higher Education, Levine analyzes the shift in goals and
     motivation of students over the last decade. The contem-
     porary student he describes is much less service/fulfill-
     ment oriented and rather is focussing on personal suc-
     cess and economic accomplishment against the
     background of an uncertain future. Levine is not a
     Christian, but his analysis is a telling critique of the lack
     of Christian input in the direction of our culture.

Mouw, Richard, *When the Kings Come Marching In: Isaiah
     and the New Jerusalem*, Grand Rapids, MI: B. Eerdmans,
     1983.
     This little book explores the relationship between Christ
     and culture, occasioned by a study of the vision of the
     Holy City, primarily as recorded in Isaiah 60. By
     discussing the main features of the Holy City, Mouw
     looks at issues such as commerce, technology, art,
     politics, race relations and the breadth of redemption in
     Christ. The book is soundly biblical and challenging to
     our preconceived notions of the Christian walk. Mouw is

Professor of Philosophy at Calvin College in Grand Rapids, Michigan, and the author of numerous books on related topics.

Smith, Gary Scott, *The Seeds of Secularization*, Grand Rapids, MI: Christian University Press, 1985.

In this more academic work, Smith examines the sources and process of secularization in a variety of fields and gives guidelines to avoid the mistakes of Christians in the past and prescriptions for the future. It is both readable and helpful in setting the context of our studies and an appropriate Christian perspective.

Tofler, Alvin, *The Third Wave*, New York: Bantam Books, 1980.

Building on *Future Shock*, written in the seventies, Tofler has done a great job of analyzing the changes in technology and the way that our lives and our world will be affected by it. While running the normal risks of futurists—will his picture accurately predict the future?—Tofler gives us an interesting point of analysis concerning the movement of society, whether he is right or wrong in his conclusions. Christian students must be aware of the way that such changes will affect future life, in order to get the long-range picture of the implications of their own contemporary decisions.

Walsh, Brian J.; Middleton, J. Richard, *The Transforming Vision*, Downers Grove, IL: Inter-Varsity Press, 1984.

An excellent introduction to the meaning of a Christian world-view written specifically for college and university students.

Wolters, Albert M., *Creation Regained*, Grand Rapids, MI: William B. Eerdmans Publishing Company, 1985.

This book emphasizes the biblical content of a Christian world-view, set in the context of creation, fall and redemption. The practical applications are very helpful as he looks at human aggression, spiritual gifts, human sexuality and dance.

Chapter 2

Education in Christian Perspective

Dominant Trends in American Education

The history of education in America is enlightening not only because it shows us a variety of changes that follow on the development of original educational ideas, but also because it shows us how we arrived at our present cultural situation. A study of education prepares us for a genuine survey of the current situation and for workable strategies of influence.[1]

The origins of education in America are unmistakably Christian. The first nine colleges in America were all begun by Christians with the intent to educate students to live a life consistent with the will of God as revealed in Scripture.[2] It usually happened this way: A group would settle in America and soon after the community was established, it would select a teacher for its youth. These teachers, unprepared and underpaid, struggled to provide education to the local citizens in whatever way they could, until an academy could be established. Formal institutions were styled after the European academy which found its roots in the ancient Greek academy.[3] When these academies reached their limits, it was time for them to get a charter and become a university. By 1862, nearly 500 colleges had been established or at least attempted. Of these, all but 21 had specifically Christian roots.[4]

Two significant points arise. First, early American Christianity had a strong commitment to the educational calling, rooted in the protestant concern for an educated clergy. Behind lay the mighty force of the Reformation, with its desire to see all believers able to accept full responsiblity before God by properly interpreting the Scripture. To fulfill this task, Reformation brothers and sisters set out on a massive educational undertaking.[5] For this they are to be applauded. On the other hand, an academy education undercut their noble purpose. Such schools were deeply committed to Aquinas' nature/grace framework. Generally speaking, this view divided up all of life between the realms of the secular and the sacred, the natural and spiritual, the public and the private, or nature and grace.[6]

In the realm of grace, Scripture is the supreme authority, and absolutely necessary if one is to gain the supernatural truth (beliefs) necessary for salvation. However, in the realm of nature, autonomous human theorizing is the supreme authority. Man need only use his reasoning power (common to all men regardless of their religious commitments) to discover the natural truths (facts) of reality. In this system the Bible was respected and studied, but only to give insight to a part of life—the spiritual. In the rest of life—the natural—people were guided by the prevailing human tradition, and the Bible was only consulted to curb excesses in the details of any particular theory. It was the common practice of the schools of the day to encourage orthodox "Christianity" and to teach the validity of Greek logic and physics at the same time, without any sense of contradiction.

This division of life between nature/grace meant that the seed of secularization was present in the school from the very beginning. If we might use the analogy of a fish bowl, we could say that into the fish bowl of the school there were introduced two fish whose task it was to take care of the affairs of the bowl, each having its specific duties. The assumption was that these two fish were compatible and that each had its own area of expertise. What the educators didn't know was that one of the fish (nature) would sooner or later eat the other (grace) and leave a school directed by autonomous human thinking.

As the times changed so did education in America. The revolutionary period of the 18th century witnessed two major impacts. The first was brought by the Revolution itself. A new nation struggling to implement a new government in a new land needed stable institutions. More and more, schools were seen as the way by which the state, not the Kingdom of God, was to perpetuate itself. To go about enlisting the schools in this holy task the state either had to seize control of the already existing schools, or start new ones. During this time,

"nonsectarian" public education was started on all levels.
There were also attempts at seizure. The classic struggle of
Dartmouth College to maintain its autonomy from the state
and the attempts of Thomas Jefferson to infiltrate William
and Mary are powerful examples.[7] But it must have been obvious that a predominately Christian citizenry would not
tolerate a "purely" secular education system, at least not yet.
That change had to come slowly or take place in new institutions.

A second powerful impetus for change was the scientific
revolution. With overwhelming new discoveries in the natural
sciences, modern science and its inductive method won the
day. Since a view cut off from Christian faith was already
functioning in the schools, it wasn't hard to replace it with a
new but similar view that seemed to do better justice to our
observations and to promise technological benefits. As state
influence and involvement increased and the new humanistic
science grew, the schools became more secular even though
individual Christians within the schools were still a positive
force. Trappings of Christianity such as prayer and Bible
reading (though more and more general), were still apparent
in curriculum. It is interesting that the Sunday school
movements came, at least in part, out of reaction to the loss of
Christian vision in the nation's secular schools.

The next major tremor was felt during the Industrial
Revolution and immediately following. The schools were
faced with two questions. First, how were they to do justice to
the growing plurality of religion, ethnic, racial, and
socioeconomic groups they encountered? Second, what was
the school's place to be in the growing Industrial Revolution?
It is easier to outline the answer to the second question first.
Schools pledged themselves to the belief in progress. Their
place was to prepare the participant for the developing industrial society.[8] In order to do this, schools became the major vehicle of the melting pot theory. Playing on the myth of
neutrality already present in educational philosophy, it was a
short step to demanding a type of practical secular uniformity
in order for the individual and nation to progress. Doing
justice to the variety of views was out of the question. This
uniformity model has governed primary and secondary
education until today.

The grip of the secular state did not tighten around education without protest. Roman Catholics were insightful enough
to see the handwriting on the wall and launched a massive

campaign for parochial schools, moving solidly back into the nature/grace schema.[9] Various religious and ethnic groups struggled with alternative educational models to preserve their identity. Christian leaders showed great concern for the dangers ahead.[10] But a radically Christian alternative did not appear, and popular Christian opinion was in support of "progress."[11] Uniquely Christian scholarship in all nontheological fields was barely in its infancy and could not contend against the juggernaut of secular education. At the university, nature was busy finishing off grace.

The Task of American Education

In this climate, a humanistic educational perspective began to blossom. The first schools of education grew out of the departments of philosophy and psychology at universities. Then came an explosion of educational ideas. Every new insight in psychology, philosophy, sociology, or economics created and continues to create a proliferation of educational writings. Education is second only to religion in the volumes of material it has produced, and, considering its rather short modern history, will probably lead in the future. In America, the bulk of writing in the 20th century has been reworked insights into how to make the present system work better. Educational giants like John Dewey articulated comprehensive systems of reform to aid the school in fulfilling its task. But what is that task?

Dewey saw three roles for education. It was to be integrative, helping the individual become part of society; equalitarian, giving each person an equal opportunity in the Democratic society; and developmental, promoting the psychic and moral development of the individuals.[12] All this was to take place in a truly democratic society, in which the school was given a sort of messianic task—to turn that society into the best community.[13] This would seem to be the logical conclusion of the secularization of education—a humanistic, utopian vision. But there was vast dissension in the humanist house. No two educators could seem to agree on the "facts" about education. And then came the radical critique of all this "liberal" thought, the individual critique from Marxist and neo-Marxist quarters. Such thinkers protest against Dewey and all others who say that education can promote integration, equalitarianism, and psychic and moral development. They claim that in a modern capitalist society, schools only integrate citizens into an economically totalitarian society. The other supposed functions of equalitarianism and development are in fact a sham. Because of the power of class interests in society, no matter how you shape the activity within the school, the result is always negative. Without radical societal transformation, even the best school will only continue the inequalities of society.[14]

Where does that leave us today? First, the only certain thing that can be said is that there is universal disagreement about every aspect of education. Everybody thinks that learning is a great idea but the "what" and "how" differ from view to view. Yet there are majority and minority reports. The majority report in American education is this: the direction of education in all its aspects is secular; that is, derived from autonomous human theorizing. Nature has finally consumed grace. Human beings are viewed as the makers of truth. It is generally agreed that the curriculum should be fairly traditional; knowledge is viewed as separate bits of rational information that need to be intellectually transmitted to the student; the method of teaching is based on behavior modification techniques and a technocratic, meritocratic testing system; students, teachers, administrators, school boards, and parents all exist in an adversary relationship with one another; and all of this takes place under the control of and in the service to the state.[15] Everything else is in the minority report—all the protests, reforms, and any alternatives. Alternative schools, free schools, open classrooms, child centered learning, progressives, liberals, neo-Marxists, and Christians all make up a chorus of critique of contemporary education; all want to make their unique contribution to distinguishing norms for education. But the question is: As Christians do we have anything vital to say?

Education: In Search of Biblical Foundations

Education is built into creation. Obviously, Scripture is full of commands to believers about education. Over and over the Lord commands us to "learn" this and "teach" that, develop "wisdom" and use "understanding," "love Him with all our minds" and "meditate on His law day and night." But do these ancient sayings carry any modern meaning in the educational context? Can we be actively involved in obediently articulating an uniquely biblical educational thrust or should we just be quiet and let the modern theorist tell us what it's all about? Let us begin to look for some answers to this question with the original marching order of God's kingdom as found in Genesis 1:26-31. As the climax of all that God had made in His very good creation, He created men and women in His image—and commissioned them with a holy task: To rule for Him over His creation/kingdom.

It can be said that God gave one overarching command to His servants for their lives in this world: to rule for Him. Although sin would disrupt the type of ruling that takes place in God's good creation, God never turned His back on His original plan. Even after sin entered the world, God has graciously sustained His image-bearers' unique task (Ps. 8), and we await His return and the final restoration when our loving service in God's good creation will be untouched by sin and endless (Rev. 22:3-5). But what is at the heart of this task of ruling, and how does it relate to education?[16]

We are given a hint in Genesis 2:15 when we're told that in order to fulfill this task "the Lord God took man and put him in the Garden of Eden to cultivate it and keep it." This tells us that humanity has been placed in an environment (the good creation) which God has lovingly arranged in such a way as to be pregnant with potential. The task of humanity is to discover how to properly unlock the potential of all that He has prepared by His powerful word (Ps. 119:89-91). In doing it properly, God is glorified and all of His servants blessed, as they, in part, become what they were meant to be. But this task of ruling by cultivating is not limited to the garden. A senior sees a beautiful coed freshman walking through the cafeteria and he contemplates cultivating a relationship with her. What does he have in mind: To take her off campus, dig a hole, throw her in it, add some manure and water and wait for her to turn green? Let's hope not. Instead, he says to himself—"There is a servant of God, created in His image, and filled with all sorts of incredible potential. I need to discover the laws of God for how to properly develop social relationships with other people in order that through obedience to those laws, I will help this other servant of God blossom into more of what God has in mind for her."[17] Well, this is what he's supposed to say. However, when sin enters any cultivating task, the cultivating isn't abandoned, but it is redirected. A radical change in belief, dependence, authority (whatever you want to call it) means that we substitute our autonomous human theories for the law of God as the directing principle for the process of cultivating.

Then the question becomes: How can I manipulate this situation so as to rip off some of this potential for my own selfish benefit. And Bingo, new "insight" is born. Just as people can be raped, so can the earth, and all in the name of some "reasonable" theory of modern science.

At this point, four educational correlaries can be made clear regarding the original command to rule. First, it is a demand for the development of a Christian scholarship. This involves image-bearers struggling together to discover what God's laws are for opening up all the various aspects of His good creation (physical, social, economic, political, recreational, etc.). Second, this process demands a broadly based educational framework, designed not only to prepare young Christian students to go on to discover more sensitive insights into God's laws, but to enable all of God's servants to see how they are each being called to be a part of this ruling for God in His Kingdom and how they can best respond obediently to various callings. Third, teachers and students need to realize that their particular vocations, as teachers and students, are part of this cultivating process. Each in his own way is called to discover and exercise the laws of God as teaching and learning take place. Both are holy tasks, and as such are no less important than any other vocations in the overall maintenance of God's Kingdom plan. Finally, in all of this, it is not just education we are demanding, but a certain type of education. As is the case with all types of education, Christian education is founded, informed, and directed by certain authoritative principles. In obedient Christian response, our principles are founded in God's Word as we find it revealed in the Old and New Testaments. This does not mean that we are developing a religious education based on faith (spiritual) and other educators are developing a nonreligious education based on objective scientific principles arrived at through human theorizing (secular). Matters of religion are not of that nature; they are universal. As a friend of mine once put it, "It's not whether to go out on a limb or not, but simply which limb am I out on, and how far out am I willing to go."[18] If Christians can't articulate a uniquely Christian vision for education, based on the uniqueness of the principles revealed in the Scripture, then calling oneself a Christian and promising to obey God's will is irrelevant. Still, God never commands us to do something that we aren't able to do.

The Effects of the Fall on Education

So what are some of these principles that will enlighten our educational perspective in a uniquely Christian way? And what are some of the key areas of education that are crying out (Rom. 8:18-27) for Christian cultivation?

The first thing to consider is that scientific theories are always related to prescientific commitments; that is, before we do science we make certain assumptions.[19] In analyzing the contribution of any education theorist we must always take into account his or her starting point and its inevitable effect on the entire system. What this means is taking scriptural insights about sin very seriously and developing a discernment that avoids the traps of oversimplification (reductionism) and distortion. Looking at Romans 1, we learn a great deal in this regard:

> The wrath of God is being revealed from heaven against all the godlessness and wickedness of men who suppress the truth by their wickedness, since what may be known about God is plain to them, because God has made it plain to them. For since the creation of the world God's invisible qualities—his eternal power and divine nature—have been clearly seen, being understood from what has been made, so that men are without excuse. For although they knew God, they neither glorified him as God nor gave thanks to him, but their thinking became futile and their foolish hearts were darkened. Although they claimed to be wise, they became fools and exchanged the glory of the immortal God for images made to look like mortal man and birds and animals and reptiles. Therefore God gave them over in the sinful desires of their hearts to sexual impurity for the degrading of their bodies with one another. They exchanged the truth of God for a lie, and worshiped and served created things rather than the Creator—who is forever praised. Amen (Rom. 1:18-25).

Here God condemns the inexcusable actions of people who, although the truth about God is apparent and available to them, suppress that truth and worship some form of idol instead. This passage has implications for the field of education, as is foreshadowed by the use of words like "truth," "knowledge," "mind," and "wise." Although the idolatry mentioned here takes the form of physical substitutions for God, the point is clear; any substitution of a created thing for the true God, even an idea of God that is less than He has revealed Himself to be, is idolatry. Hence, this idolatry can take on many forms. The variety of humanistic viewpoints which compete in education today are witness to this. Although these vary in many details, they do hold one thing in common. They are all attempts to give meaning to life by relating all of life to a principle or fixed starting point within created reality (organic functioning, economic realities, emotional potential, cognitive abilities). Once such a starting point has been assumed and an "idol" erected, it becomes the means by which to understand all of life (including education). All textbooks, teaching methods, teachers, and children must bow down before it. Anything in education that is going to be worthwhile, effective, proper, or just plain meaningful, must be adjusted to it. All of this is discovered, of course, by the autonomous human mind. By the use of a "value-free" methodology, social scientists (educators included) think that they have discovered the main-spring of human conduct. And, although they all differ from each other, each claims to have used "the facts, and nothing but the facts." But as Ernst Cassirer points out in his *Essay on Man*:

> Their interpretation of the empirical evidence contains from the very start an arbitrary assumption and this arbitrariness becomes more and more obvious as the theory proceeds and takes on a more elaborate and sophisticated aspect. Nietszche proclaims the will to power, Freud signalizes the sexual instinct, Marx enthrones the economic instinct. Each theory becomes a Procrustean bed on which the empirical facts are stretched to fit a preconceived pattern.[20]

It's not that these great thinkers are maliciously distorting the truth or simply fantasizing. In fact, they do begin with reality—something within the created order that gives a certain meaning to whatever the field being studied. Once this faith is established, the suppression of the truth follows. Instead of reality (creation) being seen in its multidimensional character, with its meaning found in its relationship to God, all facts are reduced in order to be seen, their meaning to be interpreted, in the context of this master principle (the idol). To critique such reductionism is a cardinal principle in the formation of a Christian perspective. It arms us to do battle with some mighty principalities and prevents us from being carried away naively by the cleverness of human systems.

At the same time, it directs us to another foundational point in a Christian view of knowledge: life is always experienced in a multidimensional unity,[21] not in broken down isolated atomistic bits of truth. When a child studies weather and seeks to understand rain, the prevailing scientific approach to education is to teach him that rain, in the final analysis, is "really only H_2O. This approach rips the truth out of its multidimensional context, reduces a child's way of seeing, and reduces his response to a minimum. At the same time, this approach assumes a theoretical commitment to how we discover and judge truth (a one-sided scientific method). It shapes the student in the likeness of its one-dimensional image, seeing him as a sort of empty computer bank that needs to be filled up with separate little bits of information. It separates the curriculum into the somewhat arbitrary and highly specialized fields of study, each having its experts, teachers, who dissect life into its smallest pieces and then arrange these pieces in accordance with the master principle. But do they print out the broader and deeper connections between the pieces? The teachers themselves have learned the bits of separated information to leave them dangling meaning-free, in order to maintain a neutrality that avoids the mixing of education with values (religion). But of course, as we have already seen, that's what they can't avoid. This whole approach is saturated with a certain meaningful lack of meaning. Even if neutrality and lack of calling for a response were possible in the school, meaning would quickly seep in from the societal context in which the school functions.[22] So we see that our views of subject matter, curriculum, and method, and our perceptions of the callings of teachers and students are dominated by prescientific commitments to how we determine the content of truth. Either the earth is the Lord's and the fullness thereof or reality is made up of separate little pieces that humanity needs to arrange to create meaning. Either we allow the truth that reality is a multidimensional unity to inform our subject matter selection, curriculum, method and view of student and teacher, or we choose some form of reductionism and cloud the truth. But, you say, isn't water really H_2O? Of course it is, but it always comes in the form of a cup of cold water given to the thirsty, or a refreshing cloudburst on a summer day, or a relaxing beat on the roof at night, or a sprinkle on a baby at baptism, or in the restoration of a river polluted by individual waste. In such ways we experience the reality of water.[23]

Redemptive Activity in Education

Christians need to develop an integral approach to education. This means using basic scriptural insights to design a comprehensive approach. This work will require effort by a community of Christian educators who are willing to trust God with all their hearts and depend on Him graciously to give light in the midst of our educational darkness. In some areas, we only know the direction to start out, or what sort of things "might" develop along the way. In other areas, we're still bumbling around in the dark waiting for God to surprise us with a burst of light. We know we will need a uniquely Christian developmental theory based on a biblically informed anthropology (the view of the make-up of humanity).[24] Without a sense of timing, trying to get educated is like trying to get a drink of water from a fire hydrant. We must know when, how, and what to teach. We will have to pray that the Holy Spirit gives teachers creativity in the development of an integrated curriculum that illuminates God's world and encourages mature response on the part of the student.[25]

Pedagogy must always educate, not indoctrinate. Students must be treated with the dignity of fellow image bearers and with the freedom that accompanies such responsibility. This may require major adjustments in the determination of roles in education. Likewise, reformation must also happen in the larger societal context in which education takes place. Without a restoration of biblical direction in the family, industry, politics, race relations, sports, social life, and everything else, we run the risk of preparing children with Christian insight who will be sacrificed to a niche in an unjust and distorted world. For this reason, sensitivity to the larger societal issues must be part of all Christian educators' agenda. As a result, Christian education needs participation in and support from a larger Christian community that takes seriously its task to develop a faithful response to all the callings given its members (I Cor. 12).

Thus far, we have not made a distinction about whether the task of being a Christian educator is something that can be done only in the context of a Christian school. Our hope is to encourage all Christian educators to fully accept their calling regardless of which context they find themselves presently (public or private). But one thing must be clear, regardless of context: the calling, and hence the responsibility, remains the same. At least at this point in American history, we are not in an either/or situation. Circumstances vary, but there remains freedom for the Christian educator that has not yet been explored. There are legal questions to deal with and a uniquely Christian political mind to develop and promote in order to see maximum freedom in education.[26]

If all this seems like a life-long task—it is. But it is not the kind of job that promises to be a burden until all the questions are answered. God protects us both from that kind of meaningless drudgery and from such prideful conceit. If our life in Christ tells us anything, it's that even our best efforts, in truth, are still only an approximation of His will. Also, we know, that when we do live in the truth, no matter how difficult, we experience the joy that is found in the Lord and nowhere else.

In Proverbs 22:6 we see the command of the Lord to "train up a child according to his own way, and when he is old he will not turn from it." The word for "train up" is related to another Semitic word which roughly means "to rub on." This word is used to explain the mid-eastern custom of parents who would rub dates and figs on the gums of their young children in order that they would develop a taste for these foods while still young. The assumption is that if your tastes are fine-tuned at a young age, you will benefit from them in your maturity. Some commentators interpret this verse as a warning against allowing a child to be instructed by his own sinful inclinations. However, it can be interpreted as a positive statement that indicates that there is a proper way to train up a child, a uniquely Christian educational perspective.

The implication for us, at a minimum, is this: The future maturity of the personhood of children is in the educator's hands. Everything they do in the educational process must be so completely saturated with the goodness of God's will, that it sets the child's taste for a type of fruitful, obedient Christian living for the rest of life. Anything less than that, cheating the children out of developing the potential of what God has planned for them to be, is sin.[27] As Christian educators our task is clear: we must be more obedient in this area of Kingdom service.

Notes

1. The following is a sketch of some of the points of interest in the history of schooling in America. For a comprehensive approach see Lawrence A. Cremin, *The American Common School, an Historic Conception* (New York: Teachers College, Columbia University, 1951) and Ellwood P. Cubberley, *Public Education in the United States* (Boston: Houghton-Mifflin, 1919, 1934) for two classic accounts. David Nasaw, *Schooled to Order: A Social History of Public Schooling in the United States* (Oxford: Oxford University Press, 1979) provides the perspective of a social historian. H. Warren Button and Eugene F. Provenzo, Jr., *History of Education and Culture in America* (Englewood Cliffs: Prentice Hall, Inc. 1983) is an excellent review by two "post-revisionists." This last book is the most readable of the four and incorporates many of the features of the others.

2. For an example of these explicitly Christian purposes, consider the "Statutes of Harvard, 1646" as found in Richard Hofstadtler and Wilson Smith, *American Higher Education, a Documentary History, Vol. I* (Chicago: The University of Chicago Press, 1961).

3. For more detail on this point see John C. VanderStelt, "The Struggle for Christian Education in Western History" in *To Prod the Slumbering Giant* (Toronto: Wedge Publishing Foundation, 1972). This very readable collection of essays by Christian scholars on a variety of educational topics is must reading for all Christian students of education.

4. These remaining 21 were state institutions and were still of a generally protestant character. The 1862 Morrill Act, with its land grants to school, promoted more state schools.

5. For more information regarding the educational efforts of the reformers see Pierre Marigue, *History of Christian Education* (New York: Fordham University Press, 1926).

6. For a detailed presentation of the nature/grace scheme and its development in western culture see Herman Dooyeweerd, *Roots of Western Culture* (Toronto: Wedge Publishing Foundation, 1979,) especially chapter 5, "The Great Synthesis."

7. For an interesting reading of these important issues see "Daniel Webster argues the Dartmouth College Case,

1819" in *American Higher Education a Documentary History, Vol. I*, and "Jefferson Plans the University of Virginia, 1800" *Ibid.*

8. This point is at the heart of the "revisionists" (Neo-Marxist) critique. For an in-depth review of this matter see "The Origins of Mass Public Education," Samuel Bowles and Herbert Gintis, *Schooling in Capitalist America* (New York: Basic Books, Inc. Publishers, 1977), or for a more complete picture of the revisionist perspective see Joel H. Spring, *Education and the Rise of the Corporate State* (Boston: Beacon Press, 1972).

9. For the history of Catholic education in America see Harold A. Buetow, *Of Singular Benefit: The Story of U.S. Catholic Education* (New York: Macmillan, 1970). Many argue that the great influx of European catholics in the 19th century was a prime motive for a watered-down, but generally protestant, public school movement. For more on this see Roy A. Billington, *The Protestant Crusade, 1800-1860* (New York: Macmillan, 1938).

10. For a review of the issues discussed at this time see Gary Smith, *Calvinism and Culture in America, 1865-1915,* (Grand Rapids, MI: Wm. B. Eerdmans, 1985), note especially chapter V, "The Clash Over Educational Ideals."

11. For an in-depth look at the significance of the concept of "progress" for that time and ours see Bob Goudzwaard, *Capitalism and Progress,* (Grand Rapids, MI: Wm. B. Eerdmans, 1979).

12. These elements, along with John Dewey's overall educational strategy, are found in what is perhaps his most famous educational work, *Democracy and Education* (New York: The Free Press, 1966).

13. For a presentation of this interpretation see Rousas John Rushdoony, "John Dewey's New Jerusalem: 'The Great Community' " in *The Messianic Character of American Education* (Nutley, NJ: The Craig Press, 1979). This work is one Christian scholar's look at many individuals who were significant in the development of American education. This book can be very helpful for the Christian student who is studying the history of education.

14. This critique, as spelled out in "Broken Promises: School Reform in Retrospect" as found in *Schooling in Capitalist America*, is a major contribution to understanding the nature of education in America. Revisionist historians are

noted for their ability to make this case.

15. For the provocative insights of a revisionist historian on the testing movement see Clarence J. Karier, "Testing for Order and Control in the Corporate Liberal State" in R. Dale, G. Esland, and M. MacDonald, eds., *Schooling and Capitalism* (London: The Open University Press, 1976). Rushdoony's *The Messianic Character of American Education* adds more on several educators' commitment to state control of education. But for an overall review of the major trends in contemporary educational thought from a Christian perspective see Brian Hill, *Faith at the Blackboard, Issues Facing the Christian Teacher* (Grand Rapids, MI: Wm. B. Eerdmans, 1982). This book is essential reading for the Christian student of education. It contains both a comprehensive review of modern educational issues, with his critique, and a scholarly attempt to develop a uniquely Christian alternative.

16. For a more complete development of this understanding of Genesis 1 see Paul Schrotenboer, *Man in God's World*, (Toronto: Association for the Advancement of Christian Scholarship, 1967). More specifically, Christian college students should be sure to read B. Frey, W. Ingram, T. McWhertor, W. Romanowski, *All of Life Redeemed* (Jordan Station, Ontario: Paideia Press, 1983). This book, written for college students, outlines the biblical foundations of a Christian world view, and in chapter 5, "Daily Obedience in the Activities of Life," speaks about what that would mean in the educational arena.

17. The idea of the "law" of God the Creator for His creation is fundamental for the development of a biblical worldview. For an excellent description of this notion and its implications see H. Evan Runner, *The Relation of the Bible to Learning* (Jordan Station, Ontario: Paideia Press, 1982), revised edition.

18. For a good illustration of the unavoidable religious nature of education, see R. McCarthy, D. Oppewal, W. Peterson, G. Spykman, *Society, State, and Schools: A Case for Structural and Confessional Pluralism* (Grand Rapids, MI: Wm. B. Eerdmans, 1981), especially chapter 5. This book is perhaps one of the best for orienting a reader to the variety of issues that are involved in thinking Christianly about education. Also, Philip Phenix, *Realms of Meaning* (New York: McGraw Hill, 1964) is an excellent analysis of the relationship of "religion" and education.

19. For a presentation of the relationship between faith and science as it has functioned in the West, see Herman Dooyeweerd, *Roots of Western Culture* (Toronto: Wedge Publishing Foundation, 1979), especially chapter 6, "Classical Humanism," and chapter 7, "A Dramatic Redirection."

20. Ernst Cassirer, *Essay on Man* (New York: Doubleday Anchor Book, 1953), p. 39, as cited in E.L. Hebden Taylor, *The Christian Philosophy of Law, Politics and the State* (Nutley, NJ: The Craig Press, 1969), note especially chapter VIII, "The Crisis in Apostate Anthropology and Social Science" for a critique of the approach of modern science.

21. Christian teachers will be especially interested in considering the strategies developed to investigate the rich diversity and intricate interrelatedness of the creation as found in Geraldine Steensma and Harro W. Van Brummelen, Ed., *Shaping School Curriculum: A Biblical View*, (Terre Haute, IN: Signal Publishing/Consulting Corporation, 1977). For more detailed analysis of the concepts of "multidimensional unity" see J.M. Spier, *An Introduction to Christian Philosophy* (Nutley, NJ: The Craig Press, 1966) or L. Kalsbeek, *Contours of a Christian Philosophy* (Toronto: Wedge Publishing Foundation, 1975).

22. It is embarrasing that, on the whole, Marxists are more persistent and insightful in pointing this out than Christians have been.

23. This point was made eloquently by Arnold DeGraaff in his tape entitled "Distinctively Christian School" (Grove City, PA: Christian Educational Services, 1973). Christian students in education will also find DeGraaff's, *The Educational Ministry of the Church* (Nutley, NJ: Craig Press, 1968), to be a very helpful book in providing an approach to a uniquely Christian educational theory.

24. For an attempt of this kind see Geraldine J. Steensma, *To Those Who Teach* (Signal Mountain, TN: Signal Publishing/Consulting Corporation, 1971). This book is the best of its kind. It is practical, helping teachers to work through real issues, yet it deals with constructing perspective in education. It is a good source of bibliographic material and is ideal for the Christian student of education. Another excellent source of this type is by Jack Fennema, entitled *Nurturing Children in the Lord* (Phillipsburg, NJ: Presbyterian and Reformed, 1978).

25. For more detail in developing an integral curriculum see *Joy in Learning*, and Geraldine Steensma and H.W. Van Brummelen *Shaping School Curriculum: A Biblical View*. Helpful resources in the area of curriculum development can also be received from the National Association of Christian Schools, P.O. Box 28, Wheaton, IL 60187 and Christian Schools International, 3350 East Paris Avenue, SE, P.O. Box 8709, Grand Rapids, MI 49508.

26. Christian teachers in the public schools will be particularly interested in the thorough studies of the issues and alternatives in American public education as found in R. McCarthy, D. Oppewal, W. Peterson, and G. Spykman, *Society, State, and Schools: A Case for Structural and Confessional Pluralism* (Grand Rapids, MI: William B. Eerdmans, 1981) and Rockne McCarthy, James Skillen, and William Harper *Disestablishment a Second Time: Genuine Pluralism for American Schools* (Grand Rapids, MI: Christian University Press, 1982). Both of these books are well researched and essential for the serious Christian student of education.

27. Jesus said, "And whoever welcomes a little child like this in my name welcomes me. But if anyone causes one of these little ones who believe in me to sin, it would better for him to have a large millstone hung around his neck and to be drowned in the depths of the sea" (Matthew 18:5 & 6).

Annotated Bibliography

Please consult the footnotes for various recommendations for further reading on the various topics discussed in this chapter. The following Christian works are necessary reading for Christians in education.

DeGraaff, Arnold H. and Jean Olthuis, editors, *Joy in Learning: An Integrated Curriculum for the Elementary School*, Toronto: Curriculum Development Centre (229 College Street, Toronto, Ontario M5T 1R4).
This workbook is a collection of lesson plans (in a general sense) for planning an integral elementary curriculum. It includes units on people's tasks in the world, the earth, plants, animals, and working and living together. It is packed with great ideas on how to teach these things, supplying extensive bibliography in each

section. The introduction is particularly helpful in understanding the authors' rationale for using an integral curricular approach. Elementary teachers will find this work helping them to better understand the teaching/learning process.

Fennema, Jack, *Nurturing Children in the Lord*, Phillipsburg, NJ: Presbyterian and Reformed Publishing Company, 1978.

Although this book is specifically about a biblical approach to discipline, it is also a helpful illustration of the implementation of a biblical anthropology (view of humanity) in the practical affairs of teaching. Even more significant is Fennema's critique of behavior modification techniques in education, which are immensely popular today. This is a very important book for all students of education, who must consider the difficult task of discipline.

Frey, Bradshaw L., William Ingram, Thomas E. McWhertor and William David Romanowski, *All of Life Redeemed: Biblical Insight for Daily Obedience*, Jordan Station, Ontario, Canada: Paideia Press Limited, 1983.

This book was written specifically for college and university students who are struggling to integrate their faith with their calling as students. The heart of this material provides the biblical foundations of a Christian world view; chapter 5 deals specifically with education and would be helpful.

Hill, Brian, *Faith at the Blackboard: Issues Facing the Christian Teacher*, Grand Rapids, MI: William B. Eerdmans Publishing Co., 1982. Brian Hill is Professor of Education and was founding Dean of the School of Education of Murdoch University in Australia. This book is a combination of several articles by Hill that were previously published in the *Journal of Christian Education* and the *Journal of Religious Education*. In addition to introducing the outside perspective of an Australian, this book is very helpful in providing an overview of many questions that face Christian teachers, especially those in public education. The book is an attempt to identify and analyze the forces involved in the process of education. The critical relationship between teacher, student and the world is the heart of the book. It is very well researched and documented.

McCarthy, Rockne, Donald Oppewal, Walfred Peterson, and

Gordon Spykman, *Society, State and Schools: A Case for Structural and Confessional Pluralism*, Grand Rapids, MI: William B. Eerdmans, 1981.

This is an excellently researched and documented account of the present state of education in America, presented from a Christian perspective. Its purpose is to raise questions about the justness of the present situation. By thoroughly analyzing the relationship between religion and education from the legal, philosophic, historical and cultural points of view, the authors attempt to outline what alternatives need to be implemented to assure religious freedom and justice for all.

Mechielsen, Jack, ed., *No Icing On the Cake*, Melbourne, Australia: Brookes-Hall Publishing Foundation, 1980.

This collection of essays is extremely helpful in understanding the importance and integrality of a Christian perspective in education, curriculum in particular. It is must reading for every student, parent or concerned Christian.

Runner, H. Evan, *The Relation of the Bible to Learning*, Jordan Station, Ontario, Canada: Paideia Press Limited, 1982 (Revised Edition).

This is another book that was written specifically for college students. Its strengths are Dr. Runner's thorough biblical and philosophical development of the topic and Dr. Bernard Zylstra's "Introduction" that gives an excellent overview of the issues related to the development of a biblical world view. This book will be invaluable for the student who seeks to achieve academic discernment and the foundational principles for thinking Christianly in the university environment.

Rushdoony, Rousas John, *The Messianic Character of American Education*, Nutley, NJ: The Craig Press, 1979.

This work is a series of nearly 30 essays by Rushdoony on various significant figures in the history and philosophy of education. Many of the essays are concerned with the state's role in education and include commentary on the work of such notables as Horace Mann, John Dewey, Edward Thorndike, and George Counts. Rushdoony's style is sometimes inflammatory but his research and insight are commendable.

Steensma, Geraldine J., and Harro W. Van Brummelen, editors, *Shaping School Curriculum: A Biblical View*,

Terre Haute, IN: Signal Publishing/Consulting Corporation, 1977.

This work is the result of the contributions of many
Christian educators. It attempts to show what curriculum might look like from a Christian perspective
and gives aids in how one goes about developing such a
curriculum. This material may be more helpful for the
secondary level teacher as it contains many suggestions
for the junior/senior high school levels. The areas
covered include: biblical studies, history, sociology,
language aesthetics, psychology, physical education,
biology, physical science, math, geography and
economics. This work provides an excellent starting
point for the teacher working to develop an integral curriculum.

Steensma, Geraldine J., *To Those Who Teach*, Terre Haute,
IN: Signal Publishing/Consulting Corporation, 1971.

Every Christian student of education should read this
book. It is an excellent introduction to the biblical principles that direct education. Steensma's main goal is to
provide "key" insights that will lead to proper decision
making in the school. Perhaps it would be best to
describe this work as an introduction to Christian
pedagogy (teaching methods). The chapters contain both
theoretical and practical insights on the unique offices
of students and teachers. They suggest guidelines for
developing meaningful nurturing of students and
responsible planning by teachers. Although the book is
introductory in nature, excellent bibliographic
materials are included in each chapter to enable study
in greater depth. If you buy only one book, make it this
one.

Vriend, John, et al, *To Prod the "Slumbering Giant"*, Toronto:
Wedge Publishing Foundation, 1972.

This book is a series of essays by a number of Christian
scholars. It was written in part as a Christian response
to the "crisis in the classroom." In addition to painting
the broad strokes of the history of Christian education
and the biblical directives that drive this endeavor, it
also contains helpful material on practical matters of
curriculum development and school organization.

Chapter 3

Sports and Athletics: Playing to the Glory of God

On a Saturday morning in late June I arrive at the ball-park anticipating the upcoming game against the Lions. The temperature is in the 70's, there isn't a cloud in the sky, and a refreshing breeze blows through the trees behind the out-field. The sunlight warms the empty playing field as the squir-rels scamper from tree to tree. What a great day to be outside enjoying the creation. We couldn't have had a better day for this championship game.

It seems too bad the season has to end today. My kids sure worked hard to get to this game. I can remember those prac-tices in early April. We would be shivering out in the rain, but no one seemed to care. I would be hitting grounders to Dan at shortstop and he would be lucky if he fielded one out of three. Now we've nicknamed him Hoover because he's like a vacuum cleaner out there. Remember Romo? The first time he came up to bat he was wearing those old baggy pants. He stood on the plate facing the pitcher with the bill of his batting helmet covering his eyes. I had to bite my finger to keep from laughing. I thought he would never be able to hit the ball. Then in the opening game against the Reds he hit a single into left field. I wonder, did he really have his eyes open? He was so shocked I thought he would forget to run to first. As he stood on first base and looked into the dugout, all I could see was a beaming face, a grin from ear to ear.

Well I'd better stop daydreaming and write out my lineup because the kids are starting to arrive.

"Hi, Coach!" "Hi, Coach!" chirp the Teree twins.

"Hi, guys. Ready for the big game?"

"You bet!"

36

"They hardly slept a wink last night," Mrs. Teree confides.

"Hey, make sure you stretch out before you start throwing. And warm up slowly. We'll need you for all six innings. That goes for everyone! Stretch out before you even pick up a ball!"

Boy, do they look excited! I guess it's not everyday you get to play in a championship game. Here comes Ray. He certainly has been a big help to me. His son "Roadrunner" has the right nickname. I can't remember seeing a ball he couldn't chase down out there in centerfield.

"Hi, Ray! How are you?"

"OK, I guess. I'm probably as nervous as the kids."

"Why don't you take the outfielders and hit them some flies. That should help you get rid of your jitters."

"Good idea, Jim."

"I want all the infielders at their positions. Let's hustle. OK, bring it to first! All right, looking' good!"

I wonder where all of Sam's players are. We're supposed to start in ten minutes and it looks like he can't even field a team. Here come Frank and Pete. I'm glad they'll be umping the game. They always do a good job.

"All right, everyone come home with it and go on into the dugout."

"Hi, Jim!"

"Hi, Sam! Good to see you. Ready for the game?"

"Well, Jim, it looks like we're in trouble. I've only got eight boys. What do you think we should do?"

"The rules say if you can't field a team you should forfeit the game, but that would be a big disappointment for the kids. It would give our team the league championship, but I would rather play the game. Maybe we can postpone it to another time?"

"There's no way you can do that," warns Frank. "League rules won't allow for a schedule change."

"Wait a minute! Could we play if I loaned you a player? . . . maybe that's not such a good idea. What do you think, Ray?"

What should he do? Should a Christian athletic coach respond in a particular way that would be different than someone who does not profess Christ as his/her Lord? How should a Christian approach sports? Is God really concerned about the outcome? Does the Bible speak to these issues? Is God interested in sports? What is sport? Does God play? Did He intend that men and women be involved in sports or is sport a distraction from God's purpose for us? If He did intend us to participate in sports then how do we glorify Him in this area?

Questions. Questions. Where do we begin? In our day super athletes play in Super Bowls and command super salaries. These superstars, worshipped as heroes, become instant "authorities" in politics, education, the economy, and the nuclear arms race. The major networks serve us a continuous diet of sports all weekend long and have specials during the week. We even have a television network which does nothing but broadcast sports twenty-four hours a day, seven days a week. Opportunities abound for men, women, and children to participate in some form of recreation. We have marathons for five year olds! Yet we cry out for more! Promoters, athletes, and the media, strive to feed our insatiable appetites.

As Christians we need to look into these issues and seek God's direction if we are to bring the light of the Gospel into this important area. We certainly cannot answer all of the questions, but we can hope to offer a place to start.

During the past 2,000 years we have been profoundly influenced by Greek thought in our view of the person. The Platonic idea that we are composed of a rational soul and a mortal body has influenced humanity for centuries. The mind, on a higher plane, is trapped within an imperfect body. This Socratic dialogue illustrates this:

> And which does the soul resemble? The soul resembles the divine, and the body the mortal—there can be no doubt of that Socrates. Then reflect Cebes: of all which has been said is not this the conclusion—that the soul is in the very likeness of the divine, and immortal, and unchangeable; and that the body is in the very likeness of the human, and mortal, and unintellectual, and multiform, and dissoluble, and changeable. Can this, my dear Cebes, be denied?[1]

This view of the body being lower than the mind establishes a false dichotomy. This dichotomy has major implications for play and sports. If the soul and mind are viewed as more noble parts, it follows that to serve Christ most effectively involves developing those areas of our lives.

As Judeo-Christian thought developed, it too often was influenced by Greek philosophy. Noll and Kelly describe this synthesis of Christianity with Greek thought:

Into disintegrating Roman civilization came a new moral, philosophical force: Christianity. To the disciples of this new belief, love and good works provided the ethical basis, and philosophy provided the prop on which Christian doctrines must rest. (It was not until the time of Aquinas, in the late Middle Ages, that a systematic theology was developed.) The early Church fathers turned to previous philosophers, especially to Plato, for a base on which to develop Christian thought. The great influence Christianity exerted in changing both personal values and the design of society can be traced in part to Greek social thinkers and philosophers from whom stemmed much of Christianity's doctrinal foundation and formal theology.[2]

Philosophy was suspicious of playful activity involving the body. Augustine maintained the prominence of the "rational soul" over body, and Aquinas believed that the image of God was lodged in the mind. The Renaissance concept of freedom gave the soul freedom, but bound the body with the lower passions. Some people maintain that even the Reformation's emphasis on work and vocation contributes to this view. At best, play was seen as unimportant and unnecessary frivolity and therefore not beneficial in serving God through work, the "highest calling." With the Enlightenment, human existence was linked to the "higher" mental functions, as articulated by Descartes' "Cogito ergo sum" . . . "I think, therefore I am."[3]

This body-mind dualism with the mind being the higher form certainly has been the most influential view of man in western society, but there are also naturalists who invert the hierarchy. The body then assumes the higher position and is viewed as more important. This thinking often manifests itself in an obsession with physicality. Physical activity, sports, and exercise assume an almost mediatorial role with the divine. [Such an emphasis on the physical has its roots in Greek thought as well (Epicurus—"Eat, drink and be merry . . ."), and develops through history to the present emphasis of behaviorism and sensuality.]

Historically, the pendulum swings back and forth between body aceticism and body worship. The view we have of the person has serious implications for how we view play. If the body is to be seen in a lower realm than the mind or soul, then playful activity is sinful, or frivolous at best. Exercise is necessary only as a means to an end. It either prepares us to be better workers or better thinkers. If the body is superior to the mind and soul, then playful activity is not only necessary but sacred.

The Bible paints a different picture of the nature of humanity. The traditional view of the church departs radically from the biblical notion of humanity. The Dutch philosopher Herman Dooyeweerd explains that "the traditional theological view of man, which we find both in Roman Catholic and Protestant scholastic works on dogmatics, was not at all of a biblical origin. According to this theological conception of human nature, man is composed of a mortal, material body and of an immaterial, rational soul."[4] Scripture portrays a whole person looked at from different points of view in relation to God. We do not have a body containing a mind and soul, but rather are integral beings functioning as a totality of body and soul. The apostle Paul's use of the word body (soma) is of special importance. As image-bearers of God, our bodies or our very selves mirror God's likeness. The body gives testimony to our likeness to God as well as our dependence upon Him" . . . "for it is precisely in the body where the imaging occurs. There the invisible God takes on visible form. At the same time, the image indicates in the strongest possible way that man, while he is like God, is also wholly dependent upon him, for a reflection is nothing in itself."[5]

What then does the Bible mean when it refers to mind, heart, soul and spirit, and how are they related to the body? To make clear-cut distinctions between these aspects of the person is impossible because they are all intertwined. The use of soul in Scripture is generally used to describe the life of man. It does not exist in and of itself, but is tied in with the rest of man and is often associated with his flesh and blood. The soul refers to man's natural and earthly life and is subject to death, in contrast to the Greek idea of the immortal soul. J.C. van Asch describes the biblical usage of soul:

> The soul is the individual life bound to matter. The soul is the breath, the pulse, the life, in distinction from death. It is a substantial unit. With death the soul stops, and it returns at the resurrection. (Numbers 23:10; Judges 16:30; Genesis 35:18; I Kings 17:21; I Kings 17:17-23). For this reason the blood is considered as the carrier of the soul (Deut. 12:23; Lev. 17:14; Genesis 9:4). The soul is inseparably bound to the body; repeatedly the Bible shows us this unity

and this conforms with the reality which we can ascertain daily. Soul is the being alive of the body. Adam did not receive a soul, but became a living soul when the breath of life was blown into him. It was Greek thought that wanted to distinguish between two separate units: soul and body. The soul, as a bird in its cage, is imprisoned in the body. The soul wants to escape from the prison cell.[6]

The Pauline use of "mind" (nous) can also be translated as understanding, level-headedness, knowledge of God. It refers to a person's thought process, which is affected by his deepest self-determination. Reformed theologian Herman Ridderbos describes it as "the determinative center of his acting."[7] Paul's use of "heart" (kardia) refers to the religious-moral quality of a person. The heart is the religious center of human existence. God declares Himself to the human heart through His revelation, and it is the response of the heart that determines if a person will believe or reject God. This religious center determines the quality of man's being and actions. Paul's use of "spirit" (pneuma), when referring to the human spirit, is very similar to his use of soul. It refers to humanity in its natural condition. When Paul says "the grace of the Lord Jesus Christ be with your spirit" he could as easily have said "with you."[8] In this case, spirit "denotes man in his natural existence approached from within."[9] Spirit is also used in another context as a direction-giving principle.

Although the body, mind, soul, and heart are marred by the effects of sin, people are still image-bearers in need of redemption. It is spirit which determines the direction a person will take, whether it is in service to the King or in defiance of Him. This direction-giving principle is described by van Asch: "Spirit is above all a direction-giving principle, it takes possession of us, it reveals itself through our body. One is governed by a spirit; it is a power which motivates us to deeds, as a breath, a storm, a wind, which drives us on to something, but above all to something which gives direction to what we do or neglect to do, especially our religious deeds."[10]

As we have seen, we are created in God's image and reflect this in our entire being. The body, soul, heart, and mind integrally comprise each person. We are not by nature neutral in relationship to God, but are influenced either positively or negatively by a direction-giving principle or spirit. "It leaves no room for any neutral sphere in life, which could be withdrawn from the central commandment in the kingdom of God."[11]

If the body is good and in need of Spirit-given direction, what are the implications for play and sports? Obviously we need to pursue playful activities in a way which will give honor to our Lord. But what direction gives honor and glory to Him? How can we discern the leading of the Spirit of Christ from the leading of a false spirit? What are the characteristics of sport which give honor to our Lord?

Play: A Good Gift from God

God created man with the desire to play; woven into the fabric of the image bearer is the desire to play. It is a gift from God which radiates the goodness found in the rest of creation. It is as much a part of a person's life as eating and sleeping. Because playfulness is a good gift from God which is a part of our creaturely make-up, we should please Him with our use of it. Scripture gives many illustrations of the joyful and celebrative ways people expressed their playful nature in thanksgiving for God's goodness. God-ordained festivals, celebrations, songs, and dances of victorious triumph all testify to His concern for our playful self-expression (Ex. 15:20; Ex. 23:14-17; Lev. 23:39-41; Jer. 31:10-14; Luke 15:25-32; I Sam. 18:7; I Chron. 15:29). Celebrative and joyful playfulness evidence God's Kingdom among His people. Such redemptive playfulness acts as a signpost of the consummation of Christ's kingdom in His future arrival (Isaiah 11:6-10; Zech. 8:3-5).

When God created the first man and woman, He placed them in a garden full of playful opportunities. Of course, when Adam was walking through the garden, he didn't come upon a super-dome with astro-turf. He found no baseball bats or tennis rackets growing from the trees. When God created people in the garden, they were not put in an environment full of opportunities to participate in sports as we know today; however, being created in God's image as His representatives, they were to govern and cultivate the creation. As God's regents, they were to discover and develop the potentialities of the creation, so that the creation would testify to the glory of God. It is in this formative power, found in the historical unfolding of the creation, that games, athletics and sports have developed. What could have been the first game? Was it hide and seek in the garden? Was the tree of life home base? What exactly is play?

Characteristics of Play

Trying to define play is like trying to catch the wind with a butterfly net. You barely catch its essence while so much more escapes. But the heart of play seems to be imaginative and creative expressiveness. *Play is a freely chosen exercise of fantasy for the purpose of having fun.* It is not utilitarian; it serves no "loftier goals" such as moral development of health, for its loftiest goal is its created purpose—frolicsome and joyful fun. Healthy, playful expressions should be adventurous, uncertain of outcome; an imaginative discovering of the many nuances in God's creation. To play means to enter into a different world, with a disposition all its own, although still a part of reality. The play world often has its own rules, such as "three strikes and you're out." This world has its own spatial limits, such as being "in-bounds" or "out-of-bounds." The play world also has its own conception of time, such as "time-in" and "time-out."

Playful activity is often full of secrets and surprises that await uncovering by a vivid imagination. A delightful tension exists because the outcome cannot be predicted. Playful activity should "wake up our imaginations" placing them on "all aesthetic alert."[12] The player becomes absorbed in serious pursuit of a non-serious activity. If the player does not play seriously the quality of play is marred. A true player never feels obligated or forced into playing by some outside pressure or ulterior motive, but expectantly chooses to enter into this imaginative world.[13]

Play takes place in dislocated space with arbitrary temporal boundaries. Sometimes these artificial spatial boundaries are encompassed in a stadium and are clearly delineated. Sometimes they are spontaneously created by an imaginative child's mind. Symbolic time is created which is no longer "uniform clock time."[14] Time is often defined in terms of periods, halves, and quarters which move much like the acts of a drama. Huizinga sums up the characteristics of play:

> Play is a free activity standing quite consciously outside "ordinary" life as being "not serious," but at the same time absorbing the player intensely and utterly. It is an activity connected with no material interest, and no profit can be gained by it. It proceeds within its own proper boundaries of time and space according to fixed rules and in an orderly manner.[15]

If the heart of play is expressiveness for the created purpose of celebrative, joyful fun in the presence of our Lord,
what are the implications for people desiring to please Christ
in this area of their lives? We who have been ransomed by our
Lord should certainly reflect the joy of our redemption when
we take part in playful events. True Christian joy should be
expressed playfully as an offering of thanksgiving to our
Lord. The style of our joy should reflect the richness of life we
share in Christ and be a taste of the celebration we will join
when Christ returns and consummates His kingdom. Our play
should express the "dancing in the street" type of joy peculiar
to those redeemed by God's grace. Sanctified joy will often be
rich with pleasure, but will contrast sharply with our
culture's pursuit of pleasure for its own sake. The captives
who have been set free will develop a style of joy as a response
of praise to their Liberator. This style is a "worked-in
aesthetic feature" of our joyful expression, ". . . colorful and
to please God with style made new."[16]

Our playful activity, unlike a verbal confession of faith,
becomes a work of art giving allusive testimony to the reality
of the Kingdom of God. This aesthetic quality of our play gives
life to our expression and direction to the style of our joy.
Michael Novak notes this aesthetic reality in his description
of baseball. "Like football, baseball is a game of aesthetic
form, a ritual elaborating some music of the human spirit.
Done well, it is as satisfying as a symphony, as moving as
Swan Lake or Madame Butterfly. People who respond
aesthetically to sports are sane."[17] The aesthetic dimension of
life is that kind of activity primarily characterized by
allusiveness. Such activity is styled by suggestion, many
possible meanings or understandings; a variety of avenues for
exploration. Concurrently, play, as standing outside of life,
reflects or alludes to happenstance in ordinary life.[18]

The player's medium for artistic expression is not the
paint and canvas of the painter or the clay of the sculpter, but
rather bodily movement. Dislocated play space becomes the
stage for the performance although an audience does not need
to be present. Some of the methods players use to act out their
presentation include running, ducking, hiding, kicking, and
jumping. Imaginative participants discover various shadings
and tones in their world of play. Fakes, deception, and
trickery expressed redemptively, uncover new hidden
elements of surprise. The legendary Jim Thorpe's secret of
running was to "show the man a leg and take it away."[19] The

"statue of liberty" and "flea flicker" plays are secretive attempts which uncover delightful "nooks and crannies" in the world of play. God smiles at His creatures as they play joyously with imagination. Activity that tries to pass as play, which is not full of creative opportunities for expression, has been raped of the fullness God intended for it. The spoil sport who robs the intended fun from a game, is like a thief who breaks into your house and steals your money. Lackluster, boring attempts at "play" are offered up to our Lord not as a soothing aroma, but rather as the abominable fire of Nadab and Abihu (Lev. 10).

From Play to Sports

After seeing God's intended purpose for play, what are the implications for games, athletics, and sport? Presently clear definitions of these three areas are almost impossible. Wenkart tries to highlight the distinctions between sports and athletics:

> Historically and etymologically, sport and athletics have characterized radically different types of human activity, different not insofar as the game itself or the mechanics or rules are concerned, but different with regard to the attitude, preparation, and purpose of the participants. In essence, sport is a kind of diversion which has for its direct and immediate end fun, pleasure, and delight which is dominated by a spirit of moderation and generosity. Athletics, on the other hand, is essentially a competitive activity, which has for its end victory in the contest and which is characterized by a spirit of dedication, sacrifice, and intensity.[20]

Sports philosophers have proposed various definitions to try to get at the distinctiveness of these areas, but without unanimity. One thing that does seem apparent is that the foundation of athletics, sports, and games is play. Kenneth Schmitz echoes this conclusion. He writes that "sport is primarily an extension of play, and that it rests upon and derives its central values from play . . . But the objectives of sport and its founding decision lie within play and cause sport to share in certain of its features the sense of immediacy, exhileration, rule-directed behavior, and the indeterminancy of a specified outcome."[21] Play becomes the soil out of which sports, games and athletics grow.

As noted earlier, it is almost impossible to clearly understand the differences between play, games, athletics, and sports. Instead of trying to describe exhaustively all of the proposed distinctions, we will look briefly at some of the essential components of game and sport that have occured as part of the unfolding process of God's creation.

Certain conditions emerge which move playful activity into the world of game. Goals become introduced which direct the players' focus to a desired end. Spatial boundaries are seen in the game of dodgeball where the "dodger" must stay inside of the circle. Time boundaries define appropriate movement in "red light, green light" because the only time the players may move is during the "green light" time. Because the goals and the rules narrow the range of accepted bodily movement, the player loses some degree of freedom. But the player freely chooses to enter into this world of game, anticipating that these goals and rules will provide a joyful experience.

The introduction of obstacles also indicates that we have entered into the game world. Obstacles provide hindrances which prevent the player from using the most efficient way of accomplishing the goal. The joy in the game is in creating tactics to overcome the obstacles and accomplish the goal. If the obstacles are ignored because the participant desires to use the most efficient method of obtaining the goal, then the game is destroyed. If the player removes the blindfold in "pin-the-tail-on-the-donkey", the entire game is ruined. It is the effort in trying to overcome the blindfold which makes the game enjoyable. Obstacles may be physical objects such as a hurdle on a track or they may be stated rules such as not being able to talk when playing charades or only moving your bishop diagonally in chess. Obstacles may also be introduced by vehicles of chance. The dice in monopoly may hinder the player from moving directly to the property space he may want to buy, or the "fortune of the cards" may prevent the player from drawing the card he needs for a full house in poker. Competition introduces obstacles which also prevent the most efficient methods of accomplishing a goal. These obstacles may be an inanimate part of the creation (trees and ponds on a golf course), an animal (as in broncobusting), an individual (as in a game of backgammon), a team (as in 'tug-of-war"), or even yourself (as you aim for your best time in running a mile). Games can also be noncompetitive as in "leapfrog" and "ring-around-the-rosie."

As we move our focus from games to sports, it is important to look at qualities which are unique to the world of sports. The goals become more complex and diverse and are more closely related to values beyond the players. A hierarchical arrangement of roles and positions emerges, such as a pitcher or a designated hitter. Rules which define spatial and time boundaries become more precise, separating the event further from "the real world." Participants freely choose to give up even more freedom because the rules they have submitted to make the boundaries clear for them. Therefore, the activity is less subject to individual expression; the rules have determined the parameters of the performance. The goals and rules are not designed to limit the effects of chance upon the outcome, but rather, they encourage physical skill and strategy. Physical exertion in performance is a necessary factor in sport not required in all expressions of game. Competition also becomes more important in the world of sport. Although many aspects of competition are included, the primary focus is individual versus individual or team against team. Because competition is such an important part of the sports world, we need to examine it in more detail.

Competition

Due to the powerful effect competition can have upon both the participants and the aesthetic quality of the performance, it is important to try to discern the healthy, created purposes of this phenomenon. At the root of competition we find cooperation. A team or individual must cooperatively agree to the stated goals and rules of the sport. In order for the sport to be played, the participants must cooperatively agree to oppose each other. If at any time during the contest one of the opponents decides not to compete, the entire event is ruined. The "quitter" chooses to stop cooperating. Healthy sporting events occur when competitors agree to play for the mutually joyful aesthetic experience it will bring to themselves and to any observers. Teams must be closely matched in performance skills and physical ability to ensure a stirring drama with an unsure outcome. A one-sided game is "a yawn" to both players and spectators. There is never any demand to watch the New York Yankees play against a Little League team. Dr. Warren Fraleigh articulates the necessary ingredients for a well-played game:

The ingredients of such a well-played and well-contested game are: (1) contestants who are well-matched in terms of performance skills and physical condition, (2) interesting and demanding strategic situations in conjunction with comparable strategic abilities among the participants and, (3) an outcome which is in doubt until the final moments of the event. The participants each utilize the very best of their abilities, conditioning and strategy. In so doing, they mutually aid each other in the cooperative achievement.[22]

At the heart of playful sports is joyful expression. At the level of play this expression is often without obstacles but can be freely demonstrated. In sports the obstacles serve as necessary hindrances in order for the expression to occur. Dr. Scott Kretchmar concludes:

It seems that hindrance from is also a hindrance for and that under this notion the compatibility of play and opposition becomes more apparent. I may be hindered from making baskets, but such hindrance allows me to express my testimony. I express myself with hindrance, not through or in spite of hindrance . . . Hindrance in this mode is not threatening, for it blocks nothing which is lacking. It is rather to be preserved because continued testimony depends upon its presence . . . The recognition is one of mutual dependence. I need the hindrance you can offer for my expression, and you need the hindrance I provide for your testimony.[23]

Hindrances serve also to help refine and improve the quality of the aesthetic experience. Opposition brings out a player's imagination and creativity. A player will develop strategy and physical skills to respond to the opposition. Julius Erving ("Dr. J.") has awed basketball fans for years with his ability to maneuver around opposing players with effortless grace to score a basket. Deception, trickery, timing, and execution become key ingredients in raising the aesthetic quality of the expression. Competition encourages the "iron sharpening iron" effect. As Christian athletes sharpen their skills, the beauty of their "art work" will be a blessing to themselves and the audience. Their Father will clap, asking the good and faithful servants for an encore.

It is crucial that we view the human hindrances of our expression not merely as objects to be overcome but rather as people. If the experience is indeed a celebrative experience, then we should be able to rejoice over our opponent's accomplishments as well as our own. Harold Myra captures this spirit. He writes:

> When we were kids, I tackled my brother in a backyard game. Years smaller than he, I grabbed his ankle and rode him thirty yards before I tripped him—Thunk!—into the hard November ground. He looked across at me, surprised. "Way to go, kid," he grunted—and the rest of that day, I was a tiger! Couldn't competitions be like that sometimes Lord? Admiring the brother who outdoes you . . . but still fighting like crazy to win? I don't have to hate the guy who beats me—I can admire his ability, if God is in me. Opponents are made in your image, too. Yet you live within me, telling me to love, even as I compete. Love people, love you, as you loved us, and died for us. Help me to take that to the ballfield, Lord.[24]

As fellow image bearers our opponents need to be affirmed and treated with dignity.

In addition to more formalized goals and rules, the increased importance of strategy and physical skill, and a stronger emphasis placed upon competition, there are other factors which separate sport from game and play. Sport usually has an historical tradition associated with it. Records are kept; heroes, legends, and dynasties emerge. John Loy observes that some sports can be considered social institutions consisting of primary, technical, managerial and corporate levels.[25] Sponsoring clubs such as the Boys Club enable youth to participate in sports. Educational institutions establish their own governmental structures like the NCAA, which rules over collegiate athletics. When the quality of the sporting expression becomes artistically significant so that an audience desires to participate, then other ancillary organizations also become very much a part of the big time sport experience. Umpire schools train their members in how to judge the game, the media helps interpret the game, owners and promoters sponsor the game, and vendors supply refreshments for the audience. The outcome of the performance now has a much broader impact than a game without an audience. Sport fans participate in the experience as they cheer, twist, laugh, squirm, cry out, hold their breath, moan, and try to climb inside the players and play the game for them. Long training becomes necessary to ensure a top-quality performance. Practice becomes a way of educating players in the necessary skills.

In the United States, big-time sporting events take the form of folk festivals. Rituals, established as part of the big game experience, become powerful symbolic expressions. Professor Edwin Cady has observed this power, commenting that "ritual serves not only to represent something, or present something aesthetically, to affect people inwardly: ritual wields genuine power; it make a difference; it makes things happen in the ordinary sensible and outward worlds."[26] Tailgate parties occur before many collegiate football games. Players dress up in their "costumes" to compete. Band-members entertain the fans, and cheerleaders encourage them. Caddy describes this big game ritual:

> Music . . . appropriate to a mass announces the "alma mater" and people begin to sing together a "credo," a "confessio," proclaiming their love and loyalty, everlasting devotion. Sometimes they join in united gesture or salute as well.[27]

Occasionally, a prayer will precede the event, casting a sacred aura over the contest. Players develop rituals which do not affect the actual game performance. Celebrative actions, such as spiking the football after a touchdown, have become widespread practices.

From the simple God-given desire to play, big time sports have developed into a form of popular art and folklore. The values of our culture are reflected in its sporting events. French anthropologist, Roger Caillois, observes that "primitive societies . . . are those under the sway of masks and possession, that is, of mimickry and ilinx. Conversely, the Incas, the Assyrians, the Chinese or the Romans are examples of ordered societies with offices and careers, where agon and alea, that is, merit and the accidents of birth, appear as elementary aspects of culture and as compliments of the game of society."[28] What kind of values are reflected in American sports? Are they consistent with the creational intention of aesthetic expressive joy in thankful celebration to the Lord of the universe? Or have they distorted God's intended purpose? We will briefly look into some responses given by leaders in the field of play and sports.

Play and Idols of Our Culture

Too often play and sport have been used to promote another more important agenda. The created purpose of frolicsome fun is not seen as a noble value in itself. Sports became the means to accomplish "higher" goals such as good health, preparation for becoming a better worker, development of moral character, economic gain, improvement of social status, ennoblement of mankind, prestige, conquering an opponent, and a platform for proselytizing—to cite a few of the many distortions. Dutch historian John Huizinga is concerned that the essential quality of play is lost if it is subjected to serve another purpose. Concerning the various approaches to a "higher goal," he writes:

> All these hypotheses have one thing in common: They all start from the assumption that play must serve something which is not play, that it must have some kind of biological purpose. Most of them only deal incidentally with the question of what play is in itself and what it means for the player. They attack play directly with the quantitative methods of experimental science without first paying attention to its profoundly aesthetic quality.[29]

Further, Dr. Robert Osterhoudt warns that the nature of play may be lost when it is subjected to another purpose. "When acting principally out of natural, biological, psychological, social, or economic motives (intents) in these activities, we are not engaging in them at their best, and as a result, not engaging in their proper forms, and, consequently, not engaging in them at all . . . for this treatment is destructive of the very spirit (that of intrinsicality) of which sport and athletics are composed."[30] By way of example, in the following statement James Michener seems to have made a fundamental mistake in elevating the values of health: "Sports should enhance the health of both the individual participant and the general society. I place this criterion at the apex of my value system."[31]

Not only has the biological side of sport been overemphasized, but in our day the economic motive is dominant. In a culture which has elevated the values of work to an idolatrous level it is not surprising to find values of the "work ethic" spilling over to contaminate play. Aristotle plants the seeds for this problem with his statement that "to exert oneself and work for the sake of playing seems silly and utterly childish. But to play in order that one may exert oneself seems right."[32] Due to the western dualistic conception of man, play has been viewed in a subordinate role to the "more significant" tasks of work. In this view, playful activity gives us the opportunity to relax and recreate in order that we can return refreshed to our work world and perform our tasks more efficiently. Stemming from an exaggerated and overbearing view of work is an obsession with progress and success. These idols have wreaked havoc in our culture, and they have misdirected our use of sport.

For example, violence has become an accepted method of actualizing the "win at all cost" philosophy. Ray Kennedy's penetrating article on violence in hockey illustrates the destructive effects of violence:

> . . . the Philadelphia Flyers have refined (hockey) into a new martial art: premeditated violence. Students of the dark craft conclude that the matter of Philadelphia's designated hitters is "strike only when behind and always at a star." "And why not?" says Schultz, the Flyer's most celebrated bullyboy. "It makes sense to try and take out a guy who's more important to his team than I am to mine. If I take out Brad Park, that's not a bad trade, is it?" Darn right it is because instead of seeing a gifted player perform, fans are forced to watch a petty mugging.[33]

Violence is not only restricted to the playing arena, it all too oftens spreads contagiously to the spectators. One such instance occured in Lima, Peru. "Because soccer is the most widely played sport in the world, it naturally provides the largest number of riots. We have seen that on May 24, 1964, in Lima Peru, nearly three hundred spectators were killed in a brawl following a disputed referee's call."[34] Bobby Clark, star hockey player for the Philadelphia Flyers sums it up well by saying, "If they cut down on violence too much, people won't come out to watch. It's a reflection of our society. People want to see violence."[35] In a society which craves violence it is no surprise that boxing draws many loyal followers. In the ring, brutality no longer is a perversion of the goal, as it is in hockey, but rather violence becomes the central focus of the "match." Two image bearers enter the ring for the stated purpose of punching and pummeling each other into submission. An even greater disgrace is that we condone and promote such brutality.

This win-at-all-costs philosophy is a glaring perversion of God's desired purpose for play. Sport becomes an extension of a highly competitive society where work-related frustrations are brought into the play arena. Vince Lombardi's law, "Winning isn't everything; it is the only thing," summarizes this idolatry. Lombardi also had some other revealing statements about football which expose this distortion. "To play this game you must have fire in you, and there is nothing that stokes fire like hate. I will demand a commitment to excellence and to victory, and that is what life is all about. This is a violent sport. That's why crowds love it."[36] A long line of coaches carry on in this direction. George Allen's, "Every time you win you're reborn; when you lose, you die a little," and Leo Durocher's, "Nice guys finish last,"[37] illustrate this dangerous direction. With this premium on winning, every coach is expected to produce the most efficient 'machines' possible for defeating the opponent. Players are reduced to being expendable parts of the mechanism. Second and third string players are valuable replacement parts in case of an injury. The joy of play becomes swallowed up by systemization and regimentation.

All too often the purpose of fielding a fine-tuned machine is because the machine will maximize profits for the owner. It is no secret that sport is big business for owner, coach, player, and supportive commercial industries. Frank Kush, when coach of the Arizona State football team, described this big business:

> My job is to win football games. I've got to put people in the stadium, make money for the university, keep the alumni happy and give the school a winning reputation. If I don't win, I'm gone. Football is pain and agony, and our kids are prepared to pay the price. Our kids get mentally prepared for violence. In a pro camp it may depend on how much pain you can take.[38]

This attitude results from a perversion of God's intention for play. Many Christians in athletics have not gone untouched by the lure of the dollar. Don Cockroft, former Cleveland Brown and highly visible Christian athlete said: "Pro football's a business, and entertainment. There's no reason we should just play for the so-called love of the game. Don't sell yourself short just because you are a Christian. Know what you deserve and go after it."[39] Rarely are Christian athletes challenged about their greed for the high salary. Gary Warner adds this to the discussion:

The sport-faith organizations have not been noted for
being overzealous in trying to eliminate greed. Their
major concern about the pro-athlete and his salary is
getting a portion of it. To be fair, a number of the pros
do give generously to their church and the organizations. Not a lot, but some. The sport-faith movement
would advise the athletes to use their money as the
Lord directs (hopefully, our way), but little attention
is given the whole matter of greed and high finance in
sports.[40]

In economics as well as other aspects of sport, the
absence of a distinctively Christian view allows dominant
cultural standards to fill the vacuum. In some places within
our society, sports have been elevated to a place of primacy.
Michael Novak describes play as follows:

The basic reality of all human life is play, games,
sport; these are the realities from which the basic
metaphors for all that is important in the rest of life
are drawn. Work, politics, and history are the il-
lusory, misleading, false world. Being, beauty, truth,
excellence, transcendence—these words, grown in
the soil of play, wither in the sand of work. Art,
prayer, worship, love, civilization: these thrive in the
field of play. Play belongs to the Kingdom of Ends,
work to the Kingdom of Means. Barbarians play in
order to work; the civilized work in order to play.[41]

In the mediatorial role that sports assume, Novak hopes that
sports will "advance the human condition beyond the state in
which we find it."[42]

Many evangelicals have a "Christianized" notion of sport:
that it can serve as a vehicle for advancing the human condition by adding to it the dimension of character-building and
self-discipline. The moral development of the players through
sportsmanship is a recurring theme. With increased participation on all levels of play, the ethical values of sportman-
ship become a popular apologetic. Competition is a tool with
which to develop courage and discipline. Warner's commitment to this philosophy is evident:

The philosophy of self-discipline must become
gospel, must be expanded, encouraged, fostered in
the early stages of our play when children begin competing . . . responsibility bred from competition is
cultivated from an inner self-discipline issuing from

a "commitment to a set of worthwhile priorities" . . .
competition—given the proper environment, emphasis, and perspective—can help build beneficial
character traits.[43]

Why is sports singled out as the great character builder?
Doesn't God's Spirit conform us to the image of His Son in
other activities as well?

Some Christians have viewed sports as an appropriate
tool with which to proselytize their neighbors. Sporting
events become platforms for evangelism. Rather than being a
delightful aesthetic expression, the sporting event is secondary to the task of "saving souls." Tom Landry, coach of the
Dallas Cowboys, articulates this philosophy with his statement: "The sports world is changing and the opportunity for
hero-worship may not exist a few years from now as it does today, so we need to use sports as long as we can to get our
message across."[44] A few ministries field teams in different
sports that travel around and compete against other teams.
Their aim is to introduce others to Christ. Their theory is that
people want to listen to athletes, and winning athletes are the
stronger attraction because losers do not attract crowds.
After a crowd has been drawn to a sporting event, the "win-
ners" are allowed to share how Jesus can make the fans win-
ners too. Using sports to do evangelism is seen to be justified
because "God uses it." Wouldn't a more appropriate response
be obedience to God's created purpose for sports? Couldn't an
aesthetically pleasing expression of life in God's joyous
Kingdom be a much more powerful witness? Some Christian
athletes have not shared the same enthusiasm in this
evangelistic process. They have felt used and manipulated.
Frank Deford, in his three-part series on "Religion in Sports"
in *Sports Illustrated*, exposes this manipulation: "The feeling
seems to be within the organizations that rather than attack-
ing the abuses in sports, the attempt is to save souls to make
sports better . . . They take the big name out of sports, use
him, and put back nothing. That's the extreme, but the danger
exists."[45] Deford underlines that there is more to being a
Christian athlete than making a public profession of faith.

God has called us to govern His good creation in conjunction with His intended purpose. We need to be obedient to our
task and act redemptively in the areas of play and sport. Only
prophetic voices can expose the destructive spirits in our
culture and offer direction for healthy, playful lives. As sport
develops further and reflects the values of our society, we will

need discernment to understand when it has taken or will take a detour from God's intended direction. We also need to be living examples of celebrative, aesthetically pleasing expressions of joy as we play and participate in sports.

The quality of our play should be an attractive sign-post that directs and entices others to the richness of God's kingdom. Our play should be imaginative, hilarious, creative expressions of thanksgiving to our good Father.

> Thus says the Lord, "I will return to Zion and will dwell in the midst of Jerusalem. Then Jerusalem will be called the city of Truth, and the mountain of the Lord of hosts will be called the Holy Mountain." Thus says the Lord of hosts, "Old men and old women will again sit in the streets of Jerusalem, each man with his staff in his hand because of age. And the streets of the city will be filled with boys and girls playing in its streets" (Zechariah 8:3-5).

Notes

1 .From *The Works of Plato* selected and edited by Irwin Edman, (New York: The Modern Library, 1956), p. 140.
2. James William Noll and Sam. P. Kelley, *Foundations of Education in America* (New York: Harper and Row, 1970), p. 6.
3. René Descartes, *Discourse*, Part IV, p. 26.
4. Herman Dooyeweerd, *In the Twilight of Western Thought*, (Nutley, NJ: Craig Press, 1980), p. 85.
5. Paul G. Schrotenboer, *Man in God's World* (Toronto: Wedge Publishing Foundation, 1972), p. 8.
6. J.C. Van Asch, *Physical Education From a Christian View of Anthropology*, K.J. Boot, translator (Dordt College, Sioux Center, IA).
7. Herman Ridderbos, *Paul: An Outline of the Theology*, (Grand Rapids: William B. Eerdmans, 1975), p. 121.
8. *The Open Bible*, New American Standard Version (New York: Thomas Nelson Bible Publishers, 1979), Philippians 4:23.
9. Ridderbos, p. 121.
10. Van Asch, p. 10.
11. Dooyeweerd, p. 89 & 90.
12. Calvin Seerveld, *An Obedient Aesthetic Lifestyle* (Stahlstown, PA: Thompson Media, August 1981) (Cassette tape).

13. Barney Steen, *Let's Play All Our Lives*, (Toronto: Institute for Christian Studies), p. 35.
14. Scott Kretchmar, "Ontological Possibilities: Sport and Play," in *The Philosophy of Sport*, Robert G. Osterhoudt, ed. (Springfield, IL: Charles C. Thomas, 1973), p. 71.
15. Johan Huizinga, *Homo Ludens* (New York: Roy Publishers, 1950), p. 13.
16. Seerveld, (tape).
17. Michael Novak, *The Joy of Sports* (New York: Basic Books, Inc., 1976), p. 15.
18. Calvin Seerveld, *Rainbows for the Fallen World* (Toronto, Ontario: Toronto Tuppence Press, 1980), p. 49, 109.
19. Novak, p. 149.
20. Simon Wenkart, "Sports and Contemporary Man," in *Motivations in Play, Games and Sports*, R. Slovenko and J.A. Knight, eds. (Springfield, IL: Charles C. Thomas, 1967), p. 27-28.
21. Kenneth L. Schmitz, "Sport and Play: Suspension of the Ordinary," in *Sport in the Sociocultural Process*, Marie Hart, ed. (Dubuque, IA: William C. Brown Company, 1976), p. 35, 45.
22. Warren P. Fraleigh, "On Weiss or Records and on the Significance of Athletic Records," in *The Philosophy of Sport*, Robert Osterhoudt, ed. (Springfield, IL: Charles C. Thomas, 1973), p. 37.
23. Kretchmar, p. 37.
24. Harold Myra, "Sports and War," *Campus Life*, April 1973, p. 29-30.
25. John W. Loy, Jr., "The Nature of Sport: A Definitional Effort," in *Sport in the Sociocultural Process*, (Dubuque, IA: William C. Brown Company, 1976), p. 61-63.
26. Edwin H. Cady, *The Big Game* (Knoxville: University of Tennessee Press, 1978), p. 89.
27. Cady, p. 87.
28. Roger Caillois, *Les Jeux et Les Hommes* (Paris: Gallimard Publishers, 1958), p. 169, 170.
29. Huizinga, p. 2.
30. Robert G. Osterhoudt, "An Hegilian Interpretation of Art, Sports and Athletics," in *The Philosophy of Sport*, Robert G. Osterhoudt, ed. (Springfield, IL: Charles C. Thomas, 1973), p. 348.
31. James A. Michener, *Sports in America* (New York: Fawcett Crest, 1976), p. 24.
32. A. Kolnai, "Games and Aims," *Proceedings of the*

Aristotelian Society, in *The Philosophy of Sport*, Robert G. Osterhoudt, ed. (Springfield, IL: Charles C. Thomas, 1973), p. 60.
33. Ray Kennedy, "Wanted: An End to Mayhem," *Sports Illustrated*, November 17, 1975, p. 20.
34. Michener, p. 531.
35. Michener, p. 530.
36. Michener, p. 520.
37. Michener, p. 520.
38. Michener, p. 324.
39. "The Sound of Money," *The Christian Athlete*, November 1974, p. 20.
40. Gary Warner, *Competition* (Elgin, IL: David C. Cook, 1979), p. 160.
41. Novak, p. 7.
42. Novak, p. 40.
43. Warner, p. 54-57.
44. Warner, p. 48.
45. Frank Deford, *Sports Illustrated*, in Warner, p. 49.

Annotated Bibliography

Cady, Edwin, *The Big Game*, Knoxville: University of Tennessee Press, 1978.
In Cady's first section, "The America Game," he looks into the powerful cultural forces operating in big time collegiate sports. He questions the popular apologetic that big time collegiate sport is educational. He assumes the reader has some background in literature and philosophy. The powerful aesthetic impact of big time collegiate sports is cleverly portrayed by Cady.
Guttmann, Allen, *From Ritual to Record*, New York: Columbia University Press, 1978.
From Ritual to Record is a well researched book describing the growth of sport from primitive games and dance to its present-day form. Guttmann attempts to define play, games, contests and sports to lay a foundation for the rest of the book. He uncovers the driving forces which have shaped the development of sport. He also examines in greater detail the influence of capitalism, protestantism, and individualism upon sports. This readable book should be required reading for anyone seriously interested in sports, physical education, or recreation. The only weakness is

Guttman's failure to see the religious nature of secularism.

Michener, James, *Sports in America*, New York: Fawcett, 1976.
This is a well-researched book by an avid sports fan. His love for sports is clear as he sends up distressing warnings that all is not well with sports in the United States. He sees the win at all cost ethic as responsible for many of the serious problems at every level from Little League to professional sports.

Warner, Gary, *Competition*, Elgin, IL: David C. Cook, 1979.
A former Fellowship of Christian Athletes member looks at his own involvements in sports and exposes some of the dangers of competition in our society. He is frank in his critique not only of the abuses of sport in America, but also of the sport-faith movements. Gary uses Jesus and the apostle Paul as positive examples of competitors to show some of the benefits of competition. Warner sees character development as the main purpose of competition in athletics.

Chapter 4

The Sociological Dilemma and Its Idols

Few disciplines have the potential to glorify God in such breadth as sociology has. Society, culture and human relations stand at the pinnacle of God's creation. In the creation story of Genesis 1 and 2, human beings are commanded to be dominion-bearers, cultivating the earth and bringing forth culture and societies.[1] As God's representatives, man and woman were given the task of unlocking the potential lodged in creation. The societies, cultures and institutions they were to form should have clearly reflected the glory of God. Therefore, the study of these things, the focus of sociology, should be a doxological activity, bringing praise to God. Ironically, however, few disciplines have been more hostile to Christianity than sociology has been. Consequently, many Christians have either avoided or condemned sociology for, as David Lyon noted in *Christians and Sociology* "it seems a threat, a pernicious dogma which promises to confuse and corrupt."[2] Is sociology to be adored or avoided? Why does this discipline evoke such diverse reactions from Christians?

To answer these questions in the space provided, we must simplify some complex issues. Nonetheless, a concerned student can find some direction here. We will begin by looking at the dilemma in which sociology currently finds itself; then we will examine the idols which have created the dilemma; and, finally, we will preview the contours of a Christian sociology. But before we begin this investigation, there are two important thoughts to keep in mind.

First, sociology as a discipline is a powerful tool. To study, analyze and understand human relationships can be of untold value. Whether the scope of that study is as focused as

60

marriage or the family, or as broad as clashing cultures or societal trends, enormous resources are available to the person who rightly understands this discipline.

Second, we live in an age of "pop-sociology" when serious and not-so-serious sociological studies appear on the best seller lists. John Naisbitt's *Megatrends*; Alvin Toffler's *The Third Wave*; Jeremy Rifkin's *Algeny*; and Landon Jones' *Great Expectations* all bring analysis and insight to our culture. But each author brings an ideological bias which focuses on one aspect of the culture and then interprets present and future developments through that perspective. Naisbitt and Toffler see everything through the lens of a glorious new age of technology. For Rifkin, the lens is bioengineering. Jones insists that the baby-boom generation will significantly affect every aspect of American culture for the next fifty years. As millions struggle with the upheavals of the current days, they turn to the best-selling pop-sociologists to try to understand society. Are they to be believed? Are their analyses accurate? Sociology is a powerful discipline. Present conditions make the sociologist's task urgent. It is in this context that we seek to gain some sense of how we should deal with sociology as Christians.

The Dilemma

In the 1980's sociology finds itself in a dilemma. Barely 100 years old as a discipline, it has been steadily increasing in prominence. Confusing sociology with social work, many students have majored in sociology, "to work with people," only to find themselves studying an abstract discipline. But the dilemma does not stem from this misunderstanding, nor even from the tendency of some sociologists to study irrelevant minutia in an age of "mega-problems." The dilemma is lodged in an internal inconsistency which has caused a crisis in sociology. While few sociologists or professors of sociology would acknowledge the depth of the crisis, it does exist. After surveying the historical development of the discipline, sociologists Ray Cuzzort and Edith King make this evaluation of its present state:

> The accomplishment of effective and "truthful" sociology is almost beyond the capabilities of human beings . . . It is better to discover at the very beginning that there are serious limitations to academic sociology and that we have to work within these limitations.[3]

Such an analysis cuts to the core of the discipline. But what is this problem that has disabled sociology? To get a better sense of this dilemma we will look at how Peter Berger, one of America's most prominent sociologists, introduces students to the study of sociology in what was in recent times one of the most widely used sociology introductions: *Invitation to Sociology: A Humanistic Perspective.*

In a stimulating introduction, Berger delimits the field to arrive at a definition. Having eliminated various misconceptions of sociology, he concludes that, "The Sociologist may be interested in many other things. But his consuming interest remains in the world of men, their institutions, their history, their passions."[4] But what is this world or society of people like that Berger urges us to study? In answering that question, Berger confronts us with one side of the dilemma. He writes:

> Society was there before we were born and will be there after we are dead. Our lives are but episodes in its majestic march through time. In sum, society is the walls of our imprisonment in history . . . Society not only controls our movements, it shapes our identity, our thought and our emotions. The structures of society become the structures of our own consciousness . . . Our bondage to society is not so much established by conquests as by collusion.[5]

While we do not wish to minimize the effect of society on the individual, we must point out that Berger's model is deterministic. In it, society is a prison which shapes and controls every aspect of who we are as individuals. He also implies at the end of the quote that we readily accept this determinism. We are no more than what society makes us. Berger himself refers to this as "gloomy determinism" and we would readily agree. This is one part of the dilemma. In describing the relation between the individual and society, one school of sociology sees the individual as totally determined by society. There would be no dilemma if determinism were accepted by all. We might not like the implications of such a view, but there would be no dilemma. The dilemma is embedded in our conviction that a deterministic model is insufficient. Berger shares this conviction.

Even though Berger has presented a compelling case for this deterministic model, he wants very much for there to be an alternative dimension. Therefore, in subsequent chapters, Berger speaks also of freedom for the individual in society.

This is the dilemma. How can a person be completely determined by society and still be free? He says:

> Freedom is not empirically available. More precisely, while freedom may be experienced by us as a certainty along with other empirical certainties, it is not open to demonstration by any scientific methods . . . In terms of social-scientific method, one is faced with a way of thinking that assumes *a priori* that the human world is a causally closed system. The method would not be scientific if it thought otherwise. Freedom as a special kind of cause is excluded from this system *a priori*.[6]

In other words, science tells us we are totally determined, but our experience tells us we are free. Even though these two positions are contradictory, Berger holds them together by saying that freedom, "is a very special category of cause, different from other causes." This is a problematic view of science and freedom. While freedom is affirmed it is at the same time excluded *a priori* from the social-scientific method. Berger states that for science to be science it must assume a closed system and therefore exclude something like freedom. This reduced view of nature relegates things outside mathematical cause and effect to another plane of reality.

But let us take one step further. What is a "very special category of cause"? If this seems confusing—it is. It seems as if there are only two choices. We can consider freedom to be a mystical quality, not a part of the real world but a figment of our consciousness. Freedom is an illusion because it cannot be verified by the scientific method. Or we can conclude that the scientific method is inadequate to explain one of the most basic elements of our experience. There seem to be two competing poles: the scientific analysis of the cause and effect relationship and the human experience of freedom.[7] Neither cause and effect nor freedom can be denied. But by excluding freedom from a closed scientific method of cause and effect, it is denigrated by the very fact it is not "science." To play freedom off against the scientific method actually puts the scientific method in a position where it doesn't belong, that is, as the determiner of truth in nature. Such a misuse of the scientific method could be called "scientism."

How could sociology get caught in such a trap? Although Peter Berger is one of today's outstanding social scientists as well as a Christian, he clearly illustrates the dilemma sociologists face. Most sociologists have chosen freedom over determinism, but in so doing they have not applied the scientific method in a totally consistent manner. Their failures engender the skepticism we saw in Cuzzort and King. The powerful tool of sociology is paralyzed by the dilemma. What brought us to this dead end? It is unlikely that God would give us a method of investigation that would contradict the life experience He decreed for us. Therefore, sin has either corrupted our use of the method or our understanding of our experience, or both. Various idols have replaced the understanding God intended for His people. In the historical development of sociology certain theories have encouraged that replacement. What were those theories? What are those idols?

The Idols

There are many reasons why sociology finds itself in this present dilemma. The causes which one posits will reflect the perspective one holds. From a Christian perspective, it is appropriate to consider those non-sacred things upon which people have built their lives. The Apostle Paul, in the first chapter of Colossians, tells us that Christ is the creator and head of all things and that in Him all things hold together. To suppose that societies, cultures and institutions hold together in some other way is to replace the truth with an idol. Using the biblical image of idols cannot adequately summarize the givens of the discipline. However, focusing upon three such idols can give us a basic perspective on the discipline as well as an explanation of why it finds itself in such a dilemma at the present time.

The first idol is that of collectivist humanism. Before defining this term, we need to see its historical place in the development of sociology.

Many authorities would rehearse the development of sociology in this way: At one time all the disciplines were part of the speculative realm of philosophy. But once the scientific method was discovered, one by one the disciplines left the womb of speculative philosophy and developed on their own as empirical disciplines guided by the scientific method. First the physical sciences and then the social sciences developed this way. Sociology as a discipline began with Auguste Comte, the French philosopher, who applied the scientific method to the study of social interactions.[8] From that point on, sociology developed. Did it take until the middle of the nineteenth century for someone to decide that the scientific method could be applied to social philosophy? While there is some accuracy to this as a descriptive development, the causes of sociology emerging when it did lie deeper than in the progressive triumph of the scientific method.

As western society moved out of the Middle Ages and broke the grip that the church had over all of life, thinkers rebelled against the dominant world view of the corrupt church. Two main alternatives appeared in the Renaissance and the Reformation. In general, the Reformation world view was an attempt to cast off the corruption of the medieval church and to recover basic biblical doctrines and practices. The Reformation world view asserted that the individual and society could be understood only in relation to God. People are subject to the laws (norms) of the Creator which govern all social relationships.[9] Because of the reality of sin, the only certain route to knowledge is God's revelation. Although this Reformation world view had a powerful effect on western civilization, in the end the west came to be dominated by the second world view.

The second world view came to prominence in the Renaissance and was further elaborated in the Enlightenment. According to the Enlightenment world view, human beings shape their own destiny (humanism). Each person has rights and freedoms and is subject to no higher authority. The key to human knowledge is the human mind, reason. The world is no longer understood as God's creation but as a self-governing system which, when studied, will reveal the nature of things.[10] The contours of the first idol are becoming apparent as we see a God-centered view of the world and sociology displaced by a person-centered view. No longer do we look to the Creator of societies, cultures, institutions and people for understanding, but instead we study the structures themselves. Instead of relying on the architect and His blueprints, we take the materials and try to construct something in the way that seems best to us. Exemplifying this Enlightenment world view, one introductory sociology text declares, "man's intelligence has created his societies."[11] While this is clearly problematic for the Christian, more belongs to the picture of this idol.

At its core the Enlightenment world view contained a sociological problem. If each person asserts his or her own autonomous identity, what can form the basis for community? As a result of this dilemma another strain of humanism developed from the Enlightenment world view during the nineteenth century: collectivist humanism. Instead of seeing the autonomous individual as the starting point for understanding society, collectivist humanism saw the autonomous collectivity (nation, race, class, etc.) as the ultimate reference point for understanding society.[12] The Enlightenment world view produced these two competing traditions, individualist humanism and collectivist humanism. One focused on the individual as the reference point, the other on the collective (nations, state, race, class, etc.) and both progressed in the nineteenth century.

However, as the century developed, the individualist tradition lost prominence. As the political effects of the French Revolution and the economic forces of the Industrial Revolution influenced society, the individualist tradition surrendered more and more ground. The rationalist tradition of individual rights, freedom and happiness, centered on the concept of self-interest, seemed inadequate for the new industrialized society. Combined with the rise of the nation-state in Europe, the collectivist tradition gained prominence.[13] Collectivist humanism became a secure foundation for social theory. Human beings were seen as ultimately social beings, and society (or state, race, class) was a self-contained framework which needed no other reference point. This was the environment that gave rise to the new discipline of sociology. The earlier scenario which pictured sociology's development as part of the progressive advance of science is therefore only partially correct. Science marched forth in a particular intellectual and social climate which affected how sociology developed.

This general overview describes how collectivist humanism became the foundation for sociology. For the Christian, that was a dark moment. Not only was the biblical world view of the Reformation displaced by the world view of the Enlightenment, but the collectivist humanism of that alternative world view became the foundation for this influential new discipline of sociology. It is with this in mind that we call collectivist humanism an idol. Instead of seeing society as created by God and structured and governed by His law, we learn that society is self-contained and in need of no other reference point.

Collectivist humanism was the soil in which sociology took root, but the scientific method guided its growth. We call it the second idol because of the status it has been given. The advances which were being attributed to science were truly remarkable. People were amazed and enthusiastic about what science could do. Therefore, it was sensible that people should try to apply the findings of science to the social realm. So dominant has the scientific method become that David Lyon has commented, "Positivism and empiricism [the reliance on the scientific method for truth or what is also called scientism] have had a big, if not biggest, influence on the development of twentieth-century sociology."[14] The scientific method became an idol when it became the guarantor of truth. Instead of truth being determined in relation to God's revelation, truth became tied to the scientific method. This became so integral to sociology that Peter Berger would write: "But within the limits of his activities as a sociologist there is one fundamental value only—that of scientific integrity."[15]

Three founding figures of sociology, Karl Marx, Emile Durkheim and Max Weber, all strove to do their sociology scientifically. But the irony cannot be missed: each one had a different philosophic foundation, and so each developed a different system.

Karl Marx is most often remembered for his political and economic thought, but he was also very important as a social thinker. His analysis of society was focused on class divisions, in particular the working class (proletariat), oppressed by the owners (bourgeois). In the end, however, the working class would throw off the oppression of the owners and create a classless society. One of the primary tools the working class possessed, Marx argued, was scientific analysis. While other classes were tied to their ideology which maintained their power, workers were not hindered by ideology. Therefore, they alone could use pure scientific analysis, and in this analysis lay their advantage.[16] Later, Marxist social analysis would provide the basis for one of the major sociological theories, conflict theory, which focused on the very real tensions and problems in society which were more than adjustments in the social organism.

Emile Durkheim, the French sociologist, used his scientific analysis to show that the individual could not be considered apart from society, and that society had peculiar qualities that came from the nature of the social organization itself.[17]

The analysis of society as an interrelated whole became the foundation for one of the most influential schools of sociology: the structural-functionalist school.

> As a frame of reference for empirical research, functional theory sees society as an ongoing equilibrium of social institutions which pattern human activity in terms of shared norms, held to be legitimate and binding by the human participants themselves. This complex of institutions, which as a whole constitutes the social system, is such that each part is interdependent with all the other parts, and changes in any part affect the others, and the condition of the system as a whole.[18]

Notice how in this definition society is a closed, organic whole. Like a giant amoeba, a change in one part causes a corollary response throughout the organism. Conflict theory reacted against this approach, but it remains dominant in twentieth century sociology.

The German sociologist Max Weber, also a giant in the history of sociology, turned his careful, detailed scientific analysis to phenomena such as the historical forms of religion so that he might be able to form reliable generalizations. Weber's study led him to conclude that all rational systems have an irrational core, and that this subjective meaning forms the basis for social action.[19] In the development of sociology, Weber's work has been developed further by those influenced by the phenomenological school of philosophy. In this perspective, human experience is bound by culture and rooted in the human consciousness. The sociologist works "scientifically" by treating human experience as data, but not by relating it to other theories of society.[20]

The purpose of reviewing these three seminal thinkers and the sociological schools which developed from them is to note the irony of their use of the scientific method. Each sociologist and tradition would claim to be thoroughly scientific, and yet each produces a different view of society. What is clear, but almost never acknowledged by sociologists, is that their use of the scientific method is intimately related to a prior notion of what the world, reality and the human person are. The scientific method is no guarantor of truth. It is just that, a method, critical for doing research. Sociologists often imply that if one rigorously applies the scientific method, he or she can arrive at an accurate understanding or reality. But the scientific method always operates within a broader frame of reference. Your world view, the paradigm by which you understand reality, will influence what you discover by the scientific method.[21] That these three theorists were each committed to the scientific method and yet each arrived at different understandings of society is a demonstration of this linkage between the scientific method and a prior understanding of the nature of reality, a world view. This does not mean we abandon the scientific method. Rather, it means that the key test of whether or not a theory of society is accurate or true depends on how accurate or true the theorist's prior understanding of reality is. Simply put, a mistaken world view will have a distorting influence on your view of society no matter how scientific your methods of investigation and analysis.

Before we leave our discussion of scientism as an idol, there are three movements in the twentieth century which have influenced our view of the scientific method and deserve our attention. The first is a response to the dilemma we just posed. If three theorists developed three different systems, unity must be found somewhere else. Therefore, as the twentieth century unfolded, rather than one school becoming dominant, commitment to a common method became dominant. Since each theorist had been committed to the scientific method, the method instead of any one theory became central for sociology. Because sociology was not accepted as an equal with the physical sciences, it strove to be radically scientific even if it had diverse starting points. This led to an eclectic approach to sociology, a synthesis of sociologies by sociologists who had nothing in common but the scientific method. This synthetic sociology (as in Talcott Parsons) coincided with the analytic philosophy of the logical-positivists such as A.J. Ayer who believed truth lay in the proper method, not in the result of that method. This extreme idolizing of the scientific method is appropriately called scientism. It has not only become the method for gaining truth but in effect is called the truth itself.

Another development in the use of the scientific method has been alluded to already. A certain intangible is involved in the dominance of the scientific method in sociology. In the nineteenth and early twentieth centuries there was a ground swell of excitement as one after another life-changing invention was discovered. This was coupled with the notion that human history was rapidly progressing toward the moment when misery and poverty would be eliminated. This mood climaxed when the technological war machine of the Allies destroyed the hideous ideology of the Nazis. Not only had science triumphed but it had won a moral victory.[22] But in the

wake of this grand triumph, as philosophers, artists,
theologians and others reflected on the victory, deep skepticism arose. What seemed to have been the pinnacle of scientific achievement had been at the same time the instrument of
death for thousands through saturation bombing and the
dropping of the atom bomb. And a deeper question: what did
this destruction and the atrocities of Nazism say about
human nature? A strong undercurrent began to suggest that
science was valuable but inadequate to explain the deeper,
more complex issues of life. This development had a stunning
influence on sociology. Until this point there had been almost
unanimous commitment to the scientific method. But with
this development, a number of new methodologies arose,
throwing sociology into a crisis.[23] Sociology became like a
tree without leaves. Until the end of World War II, sociology's
commitment to science was like the trunk of that tree. But
since then, sociology has branched out in many directions.
The scientific method continued to be very important, central
in fact. However, attention has shifted to the branches. What
is their commonality? Where are the leaves? It is this situation which caused sociologists Cuzzort and King to despair
about whether or not we can really know anything
sociologically.

One further development is important. In the late sixties
a movement arose which had a dual focus. The movement
known as radical sociology challenged the scientific neutrality of professional sociologists and claimed that the only purpose for radical sociology was to inform radical activism.
Coming out of the upheaval of the sixties, the radical school
asserted that sociologists who claimed to be neutral and
scientific were actually affirming the status quo by not critiquing it.[24] While not sharing the neo-Marxist perspective,
Christians should appreciate this unmasking of the
sociologist's presumed neutrality.

Both because of its internal inconsistencies and its unac-
ceptability as a replacement for revealed truth, the scientific
method is unable to serve as a foundation for sociology. It is
in fact an idol. Scientific investigation is a crucial tool for
sociological investigation, but only when it functions within
the broader framework of a biblical world view and when it
seeks consistency with God's laws for the social realm. Having examined two idols of sociology, collectivist humanism
and the scientific method, we now turn our attention to a
third idol, which like the other two, has a wide impact on

society, but is particularly problematic for sociology.

The third idol is the dichotomy between the sacred and the secular. Simply stated, those who worship this idol believe that there are certain areas of life that belong to the religious or sacred realm, and others that belong to the "objective," "neutral" or secular realm.[25] Our earlier critique of the idol of scientism shows this to be a mistaken notion. Our discussion has shown how the religious foundations or world views underlying sociology have engendered substantial inner tensions. In addition, because of a sacred-secular split, which assumes the neutrality of the scientific method, religion was either a subjective matter unrelated to sociology or considered as an object of sociological investigation. Christians are especially culpable for allowing such a split to be perpetuated.

One can only speculate about what might have been the result of a strong, informed Christian challenge to the presumed neutrality of sociology. Christians have been largely silent as secular philosophies have shaped the discipline of sociology. As a result, the Christian studying sociology today faces two problems caused by this sacred-secular idol. First, traditional sociologists will frequently tell the young Christian student that his or her faith is a private matter and should have no bearing on his or her study of sociology. Furthermore, some Christians affirm this privatism, while others will say, "A Christian has no business being involved in such a secular or worldly pursuit."

The effect of this idol has been devastating: it almost seems inappropriate to speak of a Christian perspective in sociology. This is reflected in two prominent sociologists' comments on the nature of religion in America. Peter Berger observes:

> This prominent public symbol (religion) was irrelevant in terms of the driving social forces and reserved its influences for the private lives of individuals.[26]

A variety of forces shaped sociology and other areas (the secular), but religion (the sacred), which reserved its influence for the individual was not one of them. Will Herberg adds:

> Secularism in America is thinking and living in a framework of reality and value remote from the religious beliefs simultaneously expressed. Every aspect of contemporary religion reflects pervasive secularism amid mounting religiosity.[27]

Herberg's assertion has been proven true over time: not only has religion had no effect on American culture but the culture has been transforming religion, manipulating it to reflect the culture. Therefore, rather than having a distinct Christian foundation for doing sociology grounded in a biblical world view, Christians have been assimilated by the culture and share the view that our religion has little to do with our sociology.

In the face of this perplexing problem we make these assertions. There is a desperate need for Christian perspectives in sociology. It is only within a consistent biblical framework that we can begin to deal with dilemmas such as were introduced at the beginning of this chapter. There is no room for Christian theoretical input as long as most Christians and sociologists are convinced of the presumed neutrality of sociology. There is no way of dealing with this presumed neutrality without challenging the idol of the sacred-secular split.

Having critiqued what we believe to be the three most basic problems or idols, of sociology, the task remains to offer some basic direction as to how we might approach this discipline in a Christian way.

A Doxology

We have been focusing on the problems that non-biblical world views have created for sociology. We must begin at the world view level. Earlier we discussed how the Enlightenment world view took prominence over the biblical world view of the Reformation. We wish to rediscover the biblical world view as a foundation to understand sociology.

The Bible teaches that society, institutions and persons can be properly understood only in relation to God. The creation-fall-redemption motif of the Bible is the basic starting point. As sociologists study society, they should realize that God created people, institutions and societies all of which are therefore in principle good. However, the fall brought distortion and damage to each of the aspects which God created. Sociology is a legitimate enterprise because it investigates a portion of God's creation. But unless sociologists acknowledge the distortion of sin in the structures of creation, they will misunderstand the nature of society. Our attention is drawn once again to the centrality of Christ. It is only through the redemption of Christ that society has the opportunity to experience renewal in its structure, which renewal can be explored and expressed in the discipline of sociology. This is not to say that non-Christians do not have genuine insights, or that simply because a sociologist is a Christian his or her work will be accurate. But only the biblical perspective allows people to overcome the distortions caused by sin.

It is also foundational to a Christian perspective to acknowledge the diversity of creation. God has created a wide variety of things, all of them subject to creation law. Because this is so, one of our primary tasks as sociologists is to discover what God's law is for social relations. How can sociology bring glory to God?

Sociology investigates the various structures which are basic to all social life, (i.e., the family, the state, friendship, etc.) and which make all social life possible. In addition sociology studies the interrelatedness of these societal structures.[28] Two major types of sociology need to be distinguished. Primary sociology studies relationships or structures where the relationship between people is primary. Structures as marriage, family or friendship exist because of the personal relationship around which they are built. For example, the structure of marriage is founded on the relationship between husband and wife.

No less important are the institutions which have a different foundation, but still contain human relationships as an integral part. A business, a school or a union has certain central functions which involve but don't focus on personal relationships. In the board room of a corporation, for example, the primary focus is business, but to the extent that there are human relationships, there is subject matter for sociology. These are the concerns of secondary sociology. All structures in God's creation that foster human interaction are the legitimate object of sociological study—sociology of work, religion, education, and law, to name a few. The sociologist does not approach these neutrally when he or she tries to penetrate the meaning of each of these structures.[29]

While method does not guarantee truth, each discipline must work out an appropriate method of empirical investigation. The social sciences have to develop research tools which most accurately investigate their discipline.

God has also established laws or norms for at least three levels of social relationships which the sociologist ought to investigate. First, there are free social relationships which involve no authority structure—neighbors, shoppers, and commuters, are examples. These relationships can be understood only by analyzing shared norms such as the common language needed for communication.

The second level is that of community and it can be identified only by the norms it shares. These shared norms link the members who are part of it (the European community, the East End or the village).

Finally, there is the level of the basic institution. There is a wide variety of authority patterns but each institution has its own law for what God intends it to be. The uniqueness and integrity of each institution must be respected by the sociologist.[30]

With these parameters in mind, we can see that sociology is an intricate discipline which covers many subjects. It seems almost to function as a philosophy because of the variety of institutions and disciplines it touches. For that reason it can also function doxologically. Sociology is a descriptive, theoretical science and it functions in a Christian way by making proper distinctions.

An example of the Christian function of sociology could be seen in regards to the family. If society is a closed system, functioning organically, an institution such as the family could be viewed with a great deal of relativity. Sociologists at the end of the sixties and beginning of the seventies were speculating that the family was becoming obsolete. With skyrocketing divorce rates, changing sexual patterns and ever increasing mobility, it seemed that the traditional American family was headed for extinction. This view continues to carry weight especially as people speculate about the effects of the new technology on the family. For many sociologists, the family as an institution will exist only as long as it is functional in society; probably it is a structure tied to Victorian culture and will eventually be obsolete.

The Christian sociologist views the family quite differently. For the Christian the family is an integral structure in God's creation. Therefore, though it may undergo change and adaptation, the family can never become obsolete. It has been established and is maintained by the law of God. No matter how a society perverts the family, as a structure it will keep recurring. For example, gay couples often wish to adopt children and begin families. Even though a gay family would be displeasing to God, the fact that gay couples want to adopt is evidence that God's structure for the family life continually reasserts itself. The fact that heterosexual individuals remarry, time after time after time, even though they may be violating the norms of faithfulness, is further evidence of the norm. No matter what distortion a particular society may bring to it, God's structure continues. For the Christian sociologist, this is the foundation for studying the family.

It is ironic that so many people see sociology as a godless discipline. Whenever sociology cuts itself off from a biblical world view, it experiences confusion and frustration. On the other hand, when people acknowledge the need for Christians to shape culture, a glorious new possibility arises. We can see society with its differentiated structure and complex inter-relatedness as an incredible testimony to the God who created, ordered and still operates with His law this magnificent social structure. To the extent that sociology opens our eyes to such a reality it indeed becomes doxology.

Notes

1. For an elaboration of this point see, Bradshaw Frey, et. al, *All of Life Redeemed*, (Ontario: Paideia Press, 1983).
2. David Lyon, *Christians and Sociology*, Downers Grove, IL: InterVarsity Press, 1975), p. 9.
3. Ray P. Cuzzort and Edith W. King, *Twentieth Century Social Thought*, (New York: Holt, Rinehart and Winston, 1980), pp. 360, 361.
4. Peter L. Berger, *Invitation to Sociology: A Humanistic Perspective*, (Garden City, NY: Anchor Books, 1963), p. 18. Our essay does not attempt a general analysis of Dr. Berger's work; we have attempted only a critique of this one introductory text.
5. Berger, pp. 92, 121.
6. Berger, pp. 122, 123.
7. Dutch philosopher Herman Dooyeweerd referred to this as the nature-freedom ground motive. For a further treatment of this topic see chapter six in his *Roots of Western Culture* (Toronto: Wedge Publishing Foundation, 1979).
8. For this scenario see: Robert Bierstedt, *The Social Order* (New York: McGraw-Hill, 1970), pp. 3-5. Also Curtis, Coleman and Lane, *Sociology: An Introduction* (New York: Bruce, 1967), pp. 4-7.
9. Alan Storkey, *A Christian Social Perspective*, (Leicester, England: InterVarsity Press, 1979), pp. 22-24.
10. Storkey, pp. 27-30.
11. Curtis, Coleman, and Lane, p. 2.

12. Storkey, p. 53.
13. Storkey, p. 53.
14. Lyon, p. 25.
15. Berger, p. 5.
16. Raymond K. Dehainant, *Faith and Ideology in Latin American Perspective*, Sondeas No. 85 (Cuernavaca, Mexico: Centro Intercultural De Documentation, 1972), p. 1-12.
17. Cuzzort and King, p. 73.
18. Thomas F. O'Dea, *The Sociology of Religion*, (Englewood Cliffs, NJ: Prentice-Hall, 1966), p. 2.
19. Storkey, p. 60.
20. Storkey, p. 68.
21. This point is thoroughly demonstrated in Thomas Kuhn's, *The Structure of Scientific Revolution*, (Chicago: The University of Chicago Press, 1962, 1970).
22. Cuzzort and King, p. 9.
23. Cuzzort and King, p. 12.
24. J. David Colfax and Jack L. Roach, eds, *Radical Sociology*, (New York: Basic Books, 1971), p. 3-26.
25. For a succinct treatment of this see Francis Schaeffer's *Escape from Reason* (Downers Grove, IL: InterVarsity Press, 1968).
26. Peter L. Berger, *The Noise of Solemn Assemblies*, (Garden City, New York: Doubleday, 1961), p. 38.
27. Will Herberg, *Protestant - Catholic - Jew* (Garden City, New York: Doubleday, 1956), p. 14.
28. Martin Vrieze, *Introduction to Sociology* (Syllabus) (Trinity Christian College, 1967), p. 21.
29. Storkey, pp. 134-135.
30. For an elaboration of these three levels see Storkey, pp. 139-145.

Annotated Bibliography

Berger, Peter L., *Invitation to Sociology: A Humanistic Perspective*, Garden City, NY: Doubleday, 1963.
While this book receives some negative critique in this paper, it is still a valuable introductory text. In addition, Dr. Berger is a Christian and one of the most respected sociologists of our time.
Cuzzort, Ray P., and King, Edith, *Twentieth Century Social Thought*, New York: Holt, Rinehart and Winston, 1980. This is an excellent introduction to the major social thinkers of the twentieth century.

Jones, Landon, *Great Expectations: America and the Baby-boom Generation*, New York: Ballantine Books, 1980.
A current example of popular sociology and the power of a broad social analysis stemming from analysis of a specific demographic group.

Lyon, David, *Christians and Sociology*, Downers Grove, IL: InterVarsity Press, 1976.
A basic introduction to some of the issues facing Christians in sociology.

Storkey, Alan, *A Christian Social Perspective*, Leicester, England: InterVarsity Press, 1979.
This is one of the best books available on the subject. It includes a good development of the interface of faith and sociology and some direction for the Christian. Its weakness is that it uses Great Britain as its subject and the reader must transfer that to the North American setting.

Chapter 5

The Confusion of Contemporary Politics

D id your vote make any difference in the last election?
Do you remember for whom you voted? Were your candidates Republicans, Democrats or Independents? Were they
endorsed by conservationists or by big business? Were they
blacklisted by the Moral Majority, the NAACP or the ACLU?
Do these categories make any difference?

Today's modern, sophisticated public relations techniques make candidates more visible than ever before, but
they frequently conceal the real person behind the campaign
masks. Moreover, a good Republican today can be far more
liberal than his or her good Democratic opponent. The views
of an Independent candidate might be more in line with traditional Republican or Democratic viewpoints—yet such a candidate isn't likely to win a significant post in our present
political situation. There is little difference between the votes
cast by the Christian politician and those of her non-Christian
colleague—so what difference does the Christian faith make?

The fact is that members of the same congregation or
prayer group can belong to either major party or even choose
opposing sides on particular issues and yet never discuss
these issues because they fail to see any relationship between
their faith and their politics.

Should the Christian commitment of a candidate make a
difference in his or her voting record? It seems obvious that
the faith commitment of most Christian officials has little if
any bearing on their political lives—so what is the relationship between Christianity and politics?

It seems today that neither voters nor politicians make a
serious attempt to relate their Christian faith to their political

decisions. Their faith actually requires them to relate the two, yet the pragmatic considerations of the contemporary political situation make working on such a relationship very difficult. It is much easier for both ordinary citizens and politicians to vote the party lines. One's choice of party line is usually determined by what embodies one's own self-interests. A politician is most likely to vote in a way that pleases the greatest number or at least appeases those who have the power and influence to provide future funding or votes for his career. In other words, instead of a political strategy that works out a Christian philosophy of life and government, even Christian politicians are likely to adopt a philosophy of pragmatism and accommodation that supports those interest groups with the most influence and to speak out on those issues that best contribute to reelection. Apparently not Christian faith, but faith in pragmatism, guides the voting of Christian men and women—whether voters or politicians. This pragmatism emphasizes the expedient, that which gains the most in votes or money or security. For too many Christians, the faith they profess is not the faith that guides their political decisions. Rather, they live by a pragmatic faith which is actually more influential in their lives and voting, despite the fact that they attend church services, weekly prayer meetings and prayer breakfasts.

Today's government and politics are dominated by basic social philosophies which divide nations. Even within nations, people are divided on the best way to decide what is just. Powerful groups and subgroups dominate American politics, asserting their own viewpoints to guard their own interests. Is there a norm for Christian politics? How can a Christian direction be discerned in the midst of so many competing points of view?

Philosophy is at the Heart of Politics

Governments throughout the world are established in a myriad of different ways: democracies, socialistic states, dictatorships and fascist nations. All of these express one of three underlying social philosophies, or some combination of them. Though somewhat simplified, the three basic social philosophies available to mankind are: individualism, collectivism, and pluralism.[1]

Individualism asserts that the individual is the center of understanding and authority in society; the individual is the basic building block of society. Within an individualistic society, social institutions are labels given to groups of individuals who associate because of common interest, for example, church, state, unions, and schools. These institutions are seen as limited, tentative and dependent on man-made contracts which by definition restrict the freedom of the individual by protecting the interests of the larger group.

Individualism views the state as a contractual creation of individuals to protect their own self-interests. The state functions to protect and preserve the "inalienable rights of individuals" and should be abolished and replaced when it ceases to do so or infringes upon those rights. Civil power is lodged in the state, but the state itself is a constant threat to the individual because it constantly expands to emphasize concern for the larger group.[2]

Collectivism, on the other hand, views the collective or group as most important. Individuals have meaning only as parts of the whole. The whole cannot be reduced to the sum of its parts, but is greater than those parts. The whole is autonomous and normative for its members.

Collectivism usually identifies all people with some particular structure in society, usually the state. The rights of the structure, or collective, are foremost, and people achieve meaningful lives only by conforming to the collective. Individuals are nothing in themselves; their meaning is derived from their role in the collective. All cultural activity centers around the collective whole and everything should enable the whole to continue.

Since collectivism usually identifies the whole with the state, the state is viewed as autonomous, and its standards are seen as unbreachable. All institutions within society are merely means to carry out the ends of the state. People find meaningful lives only in conformity to the state which epitomizes the collective whole. Individuals and sections of the society are granted important roles and authority by the state but only in a provisional and temporary way to enable a healthy collective in the end.[3]

Pluralism is a third viewpoint which maintains that an individual is by nature a social creature always involved in a number of social relationships. Pluralism is not a compromise between individualism and collectivism; rather, it emphasizes that people can never be reduced to mere individuals or merely some small part of a whole. Pluralism rejects the idea of the primacy of an individual standing apart

tunately, that a persuasive interest group must be behind it, or such a group must be organized.

The strength of interest groups rests in several factors. The group's size is important. The larger the constituency it represents, the more easily it will get its way. The respect or authority of an interest group may give it access to politicians which is not available to others. The urgency (real or perceived) of the cause, and so the motivation and unity of a group contributes to its influence by enabling it to mobilize its members. Finally, the financial strength of an interest group is probably its single most important resource. With sufficient monies, a group can hire researchers and lobbyists; it can conduct opinion campaigns and make beneficial campaign contributions. A small but wealthy interest group will be heard if it is effectively organized.[7] However, larger groups also have financial strength, because of their numbers.

The competition between interest groups working against each other is a new form of checks and balances. As consumer groups gain strength and see more safety measures made into law, the manufacturer groups strengthen to combat them. As big business groups seek freedom from restraint in their development (deregulation), the ecological groups grow in the effort to guard our air, water and natural resources. In the past, ideological and party motivations formed the platform from which officials operated; they can be seen as operating from the position of a certain interest group or in reaction to another. Officials from industrial states oppose agricultural interests and those from agricultural states support measures to tax industry. Rather than judging issues on their own merits, decisions are made based on the strength of interest groups involved with those issues.

There are many issues today which are decided because of the strength of interest groups involved in the debate. The military-industry interest groups wield a great amount of influence because of their direct and indirect financial strength. Elected officials would be hesitant to vote against defense measures simply because of the strength of the industrial interest groups, but even more so because of the millions of jobs directly or indirectly affected by these industries. In this way, the effects of a military build-up on world peace and power balances become of little importance.

The merits of the registration and monitoring of handguns is not considered adequately because of the strength of the National Rifle Association and its opposition to gun control of

any kind. The great number of jobs related to the auto industry make the interest groups related to that industry a
force to be reckoned with.

Yet it took the strength of the civil rights movement and
its associated political interest groups to correct the blatant
mistreatment of millions of black Americans. In these and
many more decisions, it can be seen that interest groups play
a major role in the way that decisions are made in our
political process.

The influences of interest groups are many and far-
reaching, and usually within the parameters of the law. The
question of whether it is appropriate for interest groups to
have such influence is another issue. Is it appropriate for a
handful of companies to influence Congress to enact trade
laws in their favor? Is it right for an interest group to per-
suade elected officials to pass laws benefiting them to the
detriment of whole segments of citizens who are not so well
organized? Is it appropriate for our government to financially
support certain industries via tax breaks and concessions
because of the political strength of their interest group? Can
we expect a fair discussion of the issues, their strengths and
weaknesses, when interest groups generously support their
political allies and use their financial support to undermine
their foes?[8] What happens to the weak and oppressed of this
nation under such a system?

When "strength" wins and not "right," our tax dollars are
put to work supporting tobacco industries our doctors condemn, and foreign competitors are forced to pay high tariffs if
they win at the competition game which they learned from us.
When campaign funds are so much needed and so hard to
find, will our candidates consider the issues involved or will
they consider who supports which issues? Will not the special
interest groups of the rich and powerful dominate those of the
poor who also seek power? Is it right to make decisions based
on pragmatic considerations like: "Who has contributed to
my campaign—what do 'they' think?"

Is there not a norm which stands beyond the pressure
brought to bear by interest groups? For the Christian, there
is. The norm is more than a pious morality that refuses campaign contributions or allows one only to express "Christian"
opinions on moral issues. This norm is the very character of
God and that of His people; the norm is justice.

A Christian Direction: Public Justice

Having examined a number of the complex factors that lie behind contemporary politics, we turn to the question: What is a Christian politician or voter to do? The Christian "solution" is not so easy as to align oneself with one or another political party; the social philosophy underlying all of the party options in the United States is very similar and each major party is made up of individuals across a broad spectrum of political perspectives. Add to this diversity the pressure of special interest groups, and it is clear that a Christian search for direction in politics faces a maze.

The governments of the world will vary in their approach to governing; a dictator in one country rules with the same authority as the majority party in another. The interests of some minorities are guaranteed by their strengths; small but wealthy associations will ably promote their causes. Varying views of humanity prompt varying views of government; when times are "good," conservatives prosper, but the liberals dominate when times are tough. In the midst of all these differences, there is a standard by which Christian men and women can measure politics. The standard is justice!

Scripture resounds with the theme of justice. One quickly recalls passages like Micah 6:8(b), "And what does the Lord require of you? To act justly and to love mercy and to walk humbly with your God"; and Amos 5:24, "But let justice roll on like a river, righteousness like a never-failing stream!" But justice is much more prominent in Scripture than the subject of isolated passages. Justice is an integral part of the character of God. In the same way that we worship Him because of His love, we revere Him because He is just. Justice is that upon which God's relationship with humanity is based—all His ways are justice (Deut. 32:4). Those who live in relationship to God must be just as well. Ultimate injustice has been dealt a crushing blow by the death of Christ for sin. In this way, we are declared just because of the blood of Christ. His life, death, resurrection and ascension established the Kingdom of Justice anticipated throughout the Old Testament (Jer. 42:1). The justice of God should be reflected in the everyday activities and relationships of life.[8]

God is just and His people are to live justly in Christ. The justice of God should be the rule by which all of our public activities are measured. That measure can be used to assess the actions of all governments no matter what social philosophy undergirds them. Justice can be used to evaluate decisions, no matter what party or political perspective promotes or praises them. Justice is a standard that allows us some measure of objectivity in assessing whether those who govern us do so rightly. However, justice is also a platform upon which Christians can base their political decisions.

In regard to the theme of justice, the Association for Public Justice (APJ) has developed a six-point statement about the meaning of justice, its roots and manifestations in politics. All members of APJ affirm:

> 1.   that any establishment of justice in the world is possible only because of God's judgement and redemption of the creation in Jesus Christ who, as King of kings, possesses all authority in heaven and on earth. Out of the power of His resurrection all authority on earth is delegated by Him as a responsible stewardship. He delegates this authority directly to institutions such as families, schools, churches and the state.
>
> 2.   that the state should have its specific identity as a territorial legal community of public justice. "Public Justice" indicates the normative calling of the state whose legitimate functions are established internally by public legal principles and limited externally by the task which God delegates directly to other social institutions. The proper task of the state is to bind together, in a public legal community, all persons, groups, and institutions within its territory.
>
> 3.   that government is the office of human authority within the political community (state) which is called by God to establish, enforce, and adjudicate laws for the sake of public justice, and the citizens of the state may, through elected representatives with a free mandate, legitimately exercise influence in legislation and in the general direction of the policies of their government.
>
> 4.   that the principles of public justice demand of government an equitable handling of the goods, services, welfare, protection, and opportunity that it controls, without penalty or special advantage due to religious, racial, linguistic, sexual, economic or other social and individual differences.
>
> 5.   that the policies of government should be founded on the recognition that the ongoing development of

human culture can thrive only in responsible freedom. Government therefore has no control of the internal life of nonpolitical communities, institutions, and organizations. Rather, it should restrict itself, in accord with the principles of public justice, to encouraging, protecting and making room for the development of the full range of cultural life, giving special attention to those minority groups or aspects of human culture which may from time to time be oppressed or in danger of losing their freedom to develop.

6. that no person or community of persons anywhere ought to be compelled by governmental power to subscribe to this or any other political creed, and that the government of any state ought to honor the conscientious objections that any of its citizens may have against a governmentally imposed obligation, provided these objections do not conflict with the demands of public justice.[10]

Justice is a term with applications in all areas of life. The APJ statement rightly defines the idea of public justice as the task of a state within its geographical boundaries—and declares that such a task is conducted with delegated or derived authority. Politicians must realize that their sphere of influence formally ends with government; leaving families, schools and churches to establish justice in their own right, on the basis of derived authority—authority delegated to humanity by God Himself. The APJ statement then interprets the meaning of 'public justice' in specific directions that are particularly pertinent in these times.

Many who read such a statement as the APJ "Basis for Vision" will bring unfortunate biases to their examination. For instance, the entrepreneurs and industrialists among us will cringe because the word "justice" reminds them of the cries of their workers during the last contract negotiations. On the other hand, hourly workers will be apprehensive because their bosses have underpaid and mistreated them and their predecessors for years in the name of "justice," citing the capital investments and risk taking that deserve a just return. We must carefully delineate the meaning of the word "justice." Shouldn't citizens of a state be permitted influence in the direction and execution of governmental policies? Shouldn't citizens be entitled to all opportunities of government without handicap or advantage given to any because of differences of religion, race, language, sex, income, or party affiliation? Shouldn't citizens be entitled to join nonpolitical associations and institutions that are free from governmental direction and are encouraged and protected by the political state? Shouldn't people be honored for their conscious differences with government—not forced to subscribe to any political perspective—as long as they don't interfere with the just rights of others? These questions point to a more fully developed Christian understanding of justice in the public sector. Using these as a platform—cannot a Christian direction be distilled?[11]

Remember that public justice is a guiding principle, not a "pat" answer to every problem. It is a direction, not a solution, for the just thing is not always as obvious as the injustice that it answers. Public justice can be used to measure the political solutions being offered. It can be laid alongside the platform of the Republicans or Democrats to see if the rule of justice is violated in any way. It can be compared to American conservatism or liberalism to check for incongruity, and it will give direction for correction. It can be the plumb-line in the midst of pressures from special interest groups of any kind—will this decision bring about justice for all or hamper it? But justice is complex; researching justice takes study and work. Justice must begin on the local and state levels in American politics and then be applied to national and international politics—justice is far-reaching.

Reflection on the meaning of justice in the public sector can be most readily seen by examining several true-to-life situations. What is the meaning of public justice in regards to local ordinances? Most municipalities have zoning ordinances which help regulate the way in which residential and industrial development take place. How should such ordinances be justly established?

Special interests should play little part in the determinations of "zones." Large landowners on the edge of town may indeed have a preference for the way their land is zoned. However, there are quite a few more factors involved than the profits certain property owners receive. How will one way of zoning affect nearby residents and property owners? Yes, if one property owner were permitted to strip-mine his property, he could become wealthy and the community tax base could improve significantly. But what will be the effects on the adjacent residential properties and the nearby farms. Will the drainage from the mining cause damage to the community water source? Public justice means that all of these factors are taken into account in the decision making process. Public justice may mean that a "good" project is by-passed in favor of greater benefits.

In the larger political arena, the concept of public justice must be applied on a national level. Is it just that farmers be subsidized directly or indirectly for harvesting crops to be used to produce medically harmful cigarettes? Is the public interest being served when the government is using tax dollars to augment the same industry that the government's Surgeon General condemns as harmful to the health of its citizenry? Public justice would, it seems, prohibit any hindrance from government in the manufacture of such a product. Individual citizens are entitled such "pleasures," so long as they are properly informed of the risks. But is it just to subsidize such an industry with public funds? Special interest groups on this subject are wealthy and powerful—they can be persuasive. The economy of whole states depends on tobacco and related industries, and so such subsidies are championed by their elected representatives—their jobs depend on maintaining the economic base of their constituency. Public justice in a situation like this necessitates solid research, solid convictions and the ability to withstand pressure from many sides.

Internationally, public justice may be championed instead of self-serving foreign policies. Public justice is not served merely by guaranteeing a continuity of our standard of living—the highest standard in the world, ever. Rather, public justice considers the other people of the world and their welfare rather than treating other nations as pawns in the process of accumulating power and wealth. Our prosperity cannot be justly maintained at the expense of other people and nations of the world.

> The United States is in a position where it can help to make a significant contribution to the resolution of some of these problems if it chooses to do so. It has wealth and power; it has a federal structure of government with many levels of government authority; it has a strong tradition of concern for individual rights. If Americans, especially those who are Christians, can rise above selfish preoccupation with their own wealth and power to go beyond a focus on individual rights to a broader conception of group rights, and give more attention to the complex issue

of human rights on a global scale, then much can be
accomplished in cooperation with other states and
peoples both within each state and among them all at
the international level.[12]

Public justice is indeed a standard by which we assess the
appropriateness of our politics. Further, it is a foundation
upon which we can build our own perspective and base our
decisions. If our concern is public justice, we can bring more
pressure to bear. Senator Mark O. Hatfield (R-Oregon) takes
the idea of public justice seriously. "What frustrates interest
groups is that the standard litmus tests are meaningless on
Hatfield. Neither his evangelical Baptist faith nor his
Republican party loyalty causes him to conform to any set
ready-made positions."[13] And we have a sense that this is how
it should be. Public justice means to examine seriously the
ramifications of all issues—how will they affect everyone involved? Public justice requires that such questions be
asked—again and again.

People today are frustrated with politics (less than half
those eligible to vote turn out in any given election). They are
searching for something else in which to place their trust.
Some have turned to science and technology as the answer to
all of the problems of humanity. Others have turned to Marx-
ism and its dream of equity among people. "If Christians do
not work together more vigorously, by the power of the
Gospel, to develop sound approaches to public justice, both
domestically and globally, then the world will very likely be
integrated and unified by other movements which, from a
Christian viewpoint, can only do tremendous injustice to individuals, groups and states."[14]

Politics must hear a Christian voice. In the midst of the
confusion, Christian politicians and voters must be heard
demanding public justice for all.

Notes

1. Rockne McCarthy, Donald Oppewal, Wilfred Peterson,
   and Gordon Spykman (Coordinator), *Society, State, and
   Schools: A Case for Structural and Confessional Pluralism*
   (Grand Rapids, MI: William B. Eerdmans, 1981), p. 14.
   These authors stand in a stream of thought and interpretation, including Leonard Boonin and Robert Horn, to which
   they ably refer. The classifications used in our essay are
   those of McCarthy *et. al.*, who adopted them from Horn.

2. McCarthy *et. al.*, p. 16.
3. McCarthy *et. al.*, p. 17.
4. McCarthy *et. al.*, p. 19.
5. Stephen V. Monsma, *The Unraveling of America* (Downers Grove, IL: InterVarsity Press, 1974), pp. 85-114.
6. Stephen V. Monsma, *American Politics: A Systems Approach* (Hinsdale, IL: The Dryden Press, 1973), pp. 192-4.
7. Monsma, *American Politics*, pp. 197-9.
8. Walter Isaacson with Evan Thomas, "Running with the PACS: How political action committees win friends and influence elections," *Time*, 25 October, 1982, Vol. 120, No. 17, pp. 20-26.
9. Bernard Zylstra, "The Bible, Justice, and the State," in *Confessing Christ and Doing Politics*, James W. Skillen, ed. (Washington, DC: Association for Public Justice Education Fund, 1982), pp. 39-42.
10. *Justice for All: The Basis and Vision of the Association for Public Justice* (Washington, DC: Association for Public Justice), pp. 3-5.
11. *Justice for All*, pp. 6ff.
12. James W. Skillen, *International Politics and the Demand for Global Justice* (Sioux Center, IA: Dordt College Press, 1981), p. 109.
13. Beth Spring, "Down Go the Abortion and School Prayer Bills," in *Christianity Today*, 22 October, 1982, Vol. XXVI, No. 17, p. 56.
14. Skillen, *International*, p. 105.

Annotated Bibliography

Calvin College, *Justice in the International Economic Order*, Grand Rapids, MI: Calvin College, 1980.
> This collection of essays from an international symposium held at Calvin College is a good source of ideas about various issues in international politics.

Dolbeare, Kenneth M., *Political Change in the United States*, New York: McGraw-Hill, 1974.
> A calculated and realistic appraisal of the possibilities and prerequisites for systematic political change in the USA.

Goudzwaard, Bob, *Capitalism and Progress: A Diagnosis of Western Society*, Toronto: Wedge Publishing Foundation, 1979.
> Must reading to understand the roots of capitalism as a political system.

Hatfield, Mark O., *Between a Rock and a Hard Place*, Waco,
TX: Word Books, 1976.
Hatfield, Mark. O., *Conflict and Conscience*, Waco, TX: Word,
1971.
These two books by Senator Hatfield are insights into
his own political life, highlighting the ways his faith has
influenced his political decisions.
Kirkpatrick, Jeane Jordan, *Dismantling the Parties: Reflection
on Party Reform and Party Decomposition*, Washington,
DC: American Enterprise Institute, 1979.
An interesting monograph about the two party system
in the USA, written by the US Ambassador to the United
Nations during the Reagan administration.
Marshall, Paul, *Thine is the Kingdom*, Hants, UK: Marshall,
Morgan & Scott, 1984.
An excellent work for Christians looking to develop a
Christian view of political life and responsibility. Mar-
shall's approach is not simplistic but a brief introduc-
tion to a deeply controversial field.
McCarthy, Rockne, *et. al.*, *Disestablishment a Second Time:
Genuine Pluralism for American Schools*, Grand Rapids,
MI: Christian University Press, 1982.
McCarthy, Rockne, *et. al.*, *Society, State, and Schools: A Case
for Structural and Confessional Pluralism*, Grand
Rapids, MI: William B. Eerdmans, 1979.
These two books in which McCarthy is a collaborator
are excellent examinations of the issue of true pluralism
in American politics, highlighting educational
pluralism.
Monsma, Stephen V., *American Politics: A Systems Approach*,
Hinsdale, IL: The Dryden Press, 1973.
A good text for learning the basics of American politics.
Monsma, Stephen V., *The Unraveling of America*, Downers
Grove, IL: InterVarsity Press, 1974.
An excellent resource for understanding the different
components of the American political system and their
roots in classical political thought. As a political scien-
tist and politician, Monsma's thoughts are of further in-
terest as he poses Christian alternatives.
Mouw, Richard J., *Politics and the Biblical Drama*, Grand
Rapids, MI: William B. Eerdmans, 1976.
Mouw, Richard J., *Political Evangelism*, Grand Rapids, MI:
William B. Eerdmans, 1973.
These two books are prodding examinations of a biblical

political philosophy, written for the Christian student.

Runner, H. Evan, *Scriptural Religion and Political Task*, Toronto: Wedge Publishing Foundation, 1974.
A foundational explanation of the political implications of a Christian world view.

Schaeffer, Francis A., *A Christian Manifesto*, Westchester, IL: Crossway Books, 1981.
A popular challenge to humanism which brings out relevant political implications despite its simplified historical data. A significant bestseller that challenges Conservative Christianity to take seriously its call to be salt and light.

Skillen, James W., ed., *Christian Politics: False Hope or Biblical Demand?*, Indiana, PA: Jubilee Enterprises, 1976.
A stimulating collection of essays explaining the Christian imperative in politics.

Skillen, James W., *Christians Organizing for Political Services*, Washington, DC: Association for Public Justice Education Fund, 1980.
A study guide for individuals or small groups that builds the case for Christian political associations.

Skillen, James W., ed., *Confessing Christ and Doing Politics*, Washington, DC: Association for Public Justice Education Fund, 1982.
A collection of essays that examine Christian political involvement from a variety of viewpoints from various authors.

Skillen, James W., *International Politics and the Demand for Global Justice*, Sioux Center, IA: Dordt College Press, 1981.
A challenging look at the international political situation from a Christian viewpoint, with interesting formulas presented as alternatives.

Chapter 6

Honoring God
in the Arts

Often I sing songs I don't believe,
I'm blasted with lies day by day
My diet of truth is pitifully lacking
Sadly, I may die of malnutrition . . .
and never notice.
Lord, we've ears that are deaf and eyes
now turned blind.
May renewal and reform be our daily work.

Don't feel like a novice as you begin this chapter on the aesthetic side of life. I want you to know that you are amazingly opinionated and set in your aesthetic ways. Daily you speak to others about your views on the aesthetic side of life.

Take this morning, for instance. Did you verbalize a grunt or a greeting to your roommate? How did you decide what to wear today?

Think a minute:

—did you simply grab what was draped over your chair from the night before?

—you haven't done wash for three weeks, right? No wonder what you're wearing looks so . . . "creative."

—perhaps you look at your wardrobe each day and dress in a manner proper and appropriate for the day at hand, very aware of propriety and social dictates.

—someone out there put on their boyfriend's favorite outfit, knowing that would please him.

—I awakened today feeling "ready to write." To express this mood I wanted to feel very comfortable and inconspicuous, to cubbyhole away in the library. Result? Peasant-style clothing in drab colors.

Can you see some of the motives for dress I've alluded to here? Priorities of ease, necessity, function, comfort, societal dictates, pleasing others and an expression of mood are just a few things bearing on one's decisions today. I wonder if there is any correlation between such values behind decision-making and what we value in the arts. Your life and style are modes of artistic expression. How you present yourself, your mannerisms and appearance are all a part of that. You are involved, you do have opinions.

Just as God cares about your devotional life, a life of godly actions, He's also concerned about your Spirit-empowered attitudes, the way that you view your world. Your outlook on the aesthetic side of life can either be God-honoring, or a foul stench to Him.

Not all of us are meant to be scholars in the area of aesthetics. First Corinthians 12 speaks both about specialization, and about being interactive supports. We are one body, with the responsibility of supporting and maintaining the diverse parts that make up that body. Paul is writing here to the Corinthians out of a concern that their lifestyles, their everyday ways, are not God honoring.

In I Cor. 12:25-26, Paul states that there should be no schisms in the body, but rather, caring for one another. If one member suffers, all the members suffer. Therefore, if anyone struggles in the area of aesthetics and artistic endeavors to be under Christ's Lordship, all of us struggle. You are bound to me in my being artist; I am bound to you in your field. For productivity and synchronization to occur within the movement of the body, we need first to confess our dependence upon each other, and our commitment to each other, for the Kingdom's sake. There has been too much of an emphasis on the uniqueness of artists and their need for independence. We have treated artists as creatures strange and difficult to understand. They are special, but no more special than a Christian in education or politics, who also sometimes need special working conditions. What artists really need is some elbow room for working and valuable accountability that will keep them moving in the Lord's direction. They need a community of believers and a community of artists.

One reason the artists need a community of believers is that they need to keep a perspective on all of life. If they are devoted to their art, they may not have the time they need to understand, for instance, current trends in education. Although artists may not feel directly affected by such trends, they will find their coworkers of the future to be educated from such perspectives. Eventually they will be affected, as they will also be affected by contemporary technological and political developments. We are dependent upon each other to maintain a godly stance in all areas of life.

Some have stated that creativity is an individual, not a communal matter: "collectivism destroys the arts."[1] This is dangerous. Of course, the Christian artist is not to be bound to worn-out illustrations for Sunday School material; however, one can overemphasize the artist's freedom. Collectivism does not destroy the arts; rather, it has been the impetus for the development of new directions. Artists and writers have always found each other at the local pub, discussing issues, naming their group, challenging each other's ideas and refining each other's work. There is no better place than within the Christian community to have a healthy collectivism and accountability—that is, "as iron sharpens iron, so one man sharpens another" (Proverbs 27:17).

We need to function as a body because we are in a battle, a battle to bring every area of life under Christ's Lordship. To flee responsibility in the artistic realm is to allow atrophy to set in that can poison the whole body. What if I decided that beginning tomorrow, I would not use my legs again; I will ride in a wheelchair. Wheelchair ramps are so easily accessible, and the handicap parking areas are the best spaces in town. Four or five years from now, when I need to quickly run from danger, I will regret my decision. So we lose our power to exercise strength in those areas of life in which we do not strive to see the Lord glorified.

We are the body of Christ, with great potential to honor the Lord in the arts. We do not come as neutral people without views on aesthetics. We need to pray for insight, for eyes to see and ears that can hear. We may have to struggle to understand the language of artistic expression. This learning experience will add wisdom to our knowledge. Webster defines knowledge as "acquaintance with facts, truths, or principles, as from study or investigation." Wisdom is defined as "knowledge of what is true or right coupled with just judgement as to action."

We are products of the scientific age. We call "truth" that which is analytical and factual. Art, however, engages us in a language toward a different kind of knowing. Its language is often a suggestive and subtle beckoning. Calvin Seerveld says it is "often couched in pre-analytic and pre-lingual media, like gestures, colors, sounds and shapes." He goes on to say that this does not indicate that it is void of knowledge content. He says that "symbolically enriched knowledge may take more time to read and unravel to see how it stands before the truth, but that is its glory, not a weakness."[2]

How are our eyes and ears to learn what for many of us is an unaccustomed way of seeing and hearing? They need training in an awareness that transcends yet includes subject and medium.

I often begin by taking a long look, and asking a few questions. What seems to be the intent of the piece's spirit? What seems to be glorified, man or God, creation or Creator? Where is hope found? Is God seen as the tyrannical oppressor of "fate"? Is there an end to the dominance of evil? Is blessing and peace the direction in which we're headed? I also ask: What do I know of the time period in which the artist worked? What do I know of the mediums of expression available to the artist? What was considered acceptable in the art of that day? Looking for a historical context and a philosophical context are both important; one should not try to create a dichotomy between creation and context. I do warn you, be very cautious with these questions; check yourself on your own responses. Feelings are not necessarily the measure of truth, or of right and wrong.

Art offends me when I feel the artist has invaded my private life. A piece that comes to mind is a painting of a woman taking a bath. I have seen many paintings of nudes that are stunning, a glory to womankind. But this painting beckoned me to peek through the murky water; this woman was not nude, she was naked. The focal point seemed to be to "see what you could see" when looking through the water. This not-so-graphic view of a woman's lower personal area, by stimulating the imagination, seemed to expose more than even a photograph would. I felt as if I didn't want to peek, but had caught myself peeking, being led to do what I did not want to do. As a woman, I felt exposed, my privacy invaded. My very emotional response was indignance.

At other times in a gallery I have felt uncomfortable about what seems to be an artist's own self-revelation. I have seen gross portrayals of the dark side of life that have caused my spirit to scream out at the ugliness. I think of the surrealistic works, the seemingly vivid nightmares, of Salvador Dali. Dali combines his mastery of technique, influenced by his study of some of the masters of European realism, with delvings into hallucinatory paranoia—quite a nightmare on canvas. Dali said of himself that he had a special sensitivity that enabled him to see in all objects meanings hidden from normal beings.[3] The essence of life and objects, according to Dali, is a nightmare, and it is explored with frightening precision. In his *Soft Construction with Boiled Beans* (*Premonition of Civil War*), for example, dismemberment, separation and agony are painted on a very dramatic sky. A muscular hand powerfully wrenching a breast seems to cut off the very nurturing side of life. As a woman I feel pain at the very image. In the lower left corner of the painting stands a small figure of a man. Is he orchestrating this entire event, or a victim? Could this be the artist himself? I cringe when I look at the painting, but I wonder if I cringe because it is so powerfully true, or because it is revelling in the "glory" of evil's present power. There is a difference. As Scripture teaches us how to look at the reality of good and evil, blessing and blasphemy, we then become seers. Over time, we develop more of an ability to move beyond medium to intent, from knowledge to God-given wisdom. Perhaps this can be a starting point of understanding for you. Learn to ask questions in humble awareness of God's glory and man's life dependency upon Him.

Art and God's World

What do the arts deal with? They deal with you the viewer and/or listener, you the participant and the world we live in, God's world. To help stretch your ideas about what may be aesthetic issues, I use the example of the historical stance we've taken towards housing for the poor, the needy, and those with physical or mental handicaps.

As America grew and developed, it often ignored the reality that the poor also joy in aesthetic obedience. Most public housing does not begin to praise our Father for the life contained within its womb (or rather, tomb). An aesthetically obedient housing project should also be held in the grip of scriptural truths, that is, that persons are made in the image of God; that we are called to love our neighbor as ourselves; and that the work of our hands must praise and honor our Father.

On a visit to Denmark I saw a sight that must cause God to clap His hands in joy. While walking home from church we came upon a beautiful high place overlooking the water; we walked on grassy paths through shaded areas to lovely dwellings. I asked who could afford to live there. My hostess let me know that this was a very effective home for mentally disturbed people. Imagine, such priceless beauty for those we might tend to put away in institutions, not "wasting" such beauty on those who can't afford it, or may not appreciate it quite on our terms. The people were allowed a great deal of freedom to roam, and surprisingly, problems were few. The workmanship was lovely, and from the brief glimpse I saw, it seemed to honor the occupants, acknowledging that they, too, are made in God's image.

Our senses have been so dulled and improperly trained that it takes us time to see the relationship between building structures and aesthetic obedience. We have pigeonholed art. When art came out of the cottage and stepped into the museum it was like a small stone was tossed into the water yet the ripple effect influences us today. Art is a part of the very fabric of life, not a museum piece set behind iron gates, four-foot-thick walls, three museum guards and a quarter inch of plexiglass. Nor is it a beautiful piece of music set behind $15.00 tickets, a suit and tie, valet parking, and for many, an uncomfortable calling for "put-on" airs when one enters the concert hall. This kind of pigeonholing is to believe we can squelch God's love and mercy.

What is Art?

What is art? What is God-honoring art?

A Christian style begins, but certainly does not end, with a right perspective on life. This comes as we look at all areas of life as Scripture illuminates them, providing discernment and direction, a perspective on the past, and a hope for the future. There is also the matter of skill development, Christian calling and historical setting. These practical givens allow for a lively variety; nuances of meaning find unique expression as they're affected by one's time in history and the talents one possesses. Our eyes should also look ahead for the Kingdom's call to future generations so that as God's corporate people we can move on up a path of joyful obedience.

We may read Romans 8:18-25 and see art as a part of our eager waiting for our redemption and His revelation.

> For the creation was subjected to frustration, not by its own choice, but by the will of the one who subjected it, in hope that the creation itself will be liberated from its bondage to decay and brought into

the glorious freedom of the children of God (Rom. 8:20-21, NIV).

As we seek a Christian direction in the arts, we are aware of suffering, the moans and groans of our present age. The God-honoring paths to walk are not easily found, but we must not avoid the challenge, for we're commanded to fulfill the role of steward and caretaker of the earth.

The creation was subjected to futility *in hope*. Sin affects all areas of life, but it will not have ultimate victory. Romans 8 also makes use of the pronoun "we": "We moan and groan, we eagerly wait for the redemption of our bodies." This is an activity we do as a community; we use our various gifts to serve in many areas, yet with an interrelatedness. The Christian artist needs the Christian community, and yes, the Christian community needs the Christian artist.

Christians in various fields may find themselves asking questions like: Which is most important? How do you do your work? Are the works what you do, or who you are? One *Peanuts* poster reads: "It doesn't matter what you believe, as long as you're sincere." Many Christian artists define their philosophy of art in a similar way: "It doesn't matter what your subject matter is or how you do your work, as long as your 'personal life' is under Christ's Lordship." Scripture has no patience with such double-minded wavering: James 2:17 says that faith without works is dead because it stands alone. How can the same mouth pronounce both blessing and cursing? How can a fountain send forth sweet and bitter water from the same location? (James 3:10). There should not be such a split between faith and actions. The idea that the works of our hands are neutral has developed over history. This misconception is intertwined with the progression of the influence of "objective" truth and scientific "laws." The Age of Reason said that meaningful existence was to be found in intellectual reasoning. Something that could not be intellectually reasoned out did not have important meaning. Thus the "spiritual," that realm of ideas outside of scientific "laws," was separated from everyday life. Those who still believed in God banished Him from the market-place, for He could not be defined in a merely intellectual way. The interactive nature of God, His voice being woven into the very fabric of creation, was ignored. Humanity was given final authority.

As belief in the goodness of humanity developed, there was little place or need for God. Educated freedom of thought was all important. William Blake said that instead of religion he wanted the truth. He was pleased that "the dark Religions are departed and sweet Science reigns."[4]

What progressively came to dominate was belief in the goodness of people, everyday common sense, and education. History's fluctuations were defined as an effort to avoid foundational truths, something that happens when reality and truth are defined by one's own perceptions. In sum: "Human reason is the only dependable guide to happiness and virtue. People are neither weak nor sinful, but essentially good when free to think."[5]

In the arts, these articles of faith were reflected in the shift from the Baroque to Rococo schools. The emphasis on reason and order which characterized the Baroque style becomes charming and whimsical in the Rococo style. In a similar way, Renaissance art emphasized formulas and reasoning, while impressionistic art was a reaction to it, placing man in a unique but subservient position to nature. It is said that the impressionists "left the constricting dependence upon the vanishing point and emphasized sheer color."[6] Stuart Davis, a pragmatist of American modernism asserts: "A picture is an independent object with a reality all its own."[7] This dramatic shift removes art from everyday life when it makes it an object with a meaning of its own.

With the advent of Franklin Roosevelt's New Deal era, hope was placed in progress. In public housing there was "issued a call for space, light, beauty, and collective order, an environment in which the varied needs of the individual are effectively reconciled with social needs."[8] This reflects partial awareness of human needs, but is directionally false as it places its hope in man alone. The housing makes the error clear.

Where have Christians been through all these changes? As an institution, the Church seemed to work hard to be secure and established. Stiffness, and a fear of the world around them restricted church people. Some even saw art as a "sensuous temptation that was dangerous to faith."[9] This blindness, along with separating Christian life from daily life paralyzed would-be and devout artisans.

Thoughts on Art for Today

Today we not only need to concern ourselves with remaining undefiled by the world (by which I mean the sinful influences on God's good creation), but we must also be cleansed of the oppression within our own house. This will not be an easy task. Our task should take the form of humble and loving service, yet speaking the truth in love. We are not to come as those with all the answers, for that would be false and offensive, but as ones willing to ask questions, to give of our energies, and to stand up for truth when we catch glimpses of it.

All has not been lost as history has unfolded. God's purposes will prevail. We need not go back to an earlier age to produce God-glorifying work. History is moving forward, and though oppressed by sin, God's ways have not been overcome. There will be a culmination and victory at Christ's coming, and God's purposes will prevail. Remember how Romans 8:18-25 says that the creation was subjected to vanity in hope. God will use even the foolish as His sounding boards; He will use stones, if necessary, to lead His victory, for all areas of life look forward to the purifying, redeeming work of Christ.

Works of non-Christian artisans have qualities that proclaim truth. Art historian H.R. Rookmaaker said: "This seems to be a matter of common grace, suggesting that God gives a special kind of grace, grace in a general sense so that good things are possible."[10] Often unbelievers have the ability to condemn evil and its hold on life. Look at Job's friends. They said to him, "Curse God and die." They were aware of sin's awful grip, but they lacked awareness of who the victor would be. Other artists' works may express hope, streams of living water, even while their eyes are blinded to the stream's source, our Lord Himself. What is lacking in these works is discernment, that step beyond seeing which has its roots in the Lord of Life. If reality is to be limited by our perceptions, then we certainly do need to despair.

Again, we need to look at our present state of affairs if we are to have "seeing" eyes for the future. Where have we lost our way? Shall we go to the museum to find where we've strayed? This, however, is quite a problem. When we banished art to the museums, it became the concern of the elite. Many good Philadelphians can relate to running up the art museum steps like Rocky. He symbolized a common man who became an overcomer. He gained fortune and fame, yet never lost the common touch, and they loved him. I once sat on the museum steps waiting for a Saturday morning opening. In that one-half hour period I saw at least six joggers plodding up and down the same steps that Rocky trod. None wanted to go inside, for in that stifling world they would feel awkward.

As art has become the concern of the wealthy, they are the

ones that determine the success or failure of a piece. I return to Philadelphia to cite an example. A statue of Rocky was placed outside the art museum for the film, *Rocky III*. After the filming, the statue remained and became quite a subject of debate. Many average Philadelphians felt the statue should remain. On the other side, the people of influence felt the piece unworthy of such a position. It is easy to guess who won the debate—the statue has been moved. This is not to comment on the quality of the work but rather on the excitement of the people who felt they had finally found some art relevant to their interests and situations.

In less advanced cultures, artistic craftsmanship was expressed in everyday tools, literally placing art in the hands of the common person. We are now at a point where the number of "do not touch" signs measures a piece's value, and the language spoken in modern pieces seems irrelevant and garbled to the average person.

A piece's true meaning becomes lost and fragmented when it is removed from the artist and his social concerns. Admittedly, bridging such gaps is difficult; yet we've begun to think that art in isolation is the norm. One of my favorite museums is the Picasso museum in Barcelona Spain; it seems to begin to bridge some of these gaps. One wanders through narrow alleys, past dingy cafes and grimy children through an archway into the world of Picasso. Then one again winds through a maze of Spanish architecture displaying the works of Picasso in chronological order. My senses were touched and awakened, my understanding of Picasso was greatly heightened in this hometown setting. It was a great effort, yet rare today, for the artisans themselves have become accustomed to such fragmentation.

As one looks at many of the works done today, one can tell by their size that they have no place in the home or cottage; they were created to be hung in a museum. All this leads many to define art as work that hangs isolated on a museum wall.

Lacking interaction with life, the artist and his work remain on a pedestal; misunderstanding has bred aloofness. This is the problem for both the artist and the viewer. Art speaks a language which has become foreign to us in this age. Artistic language, free from logical consistency or imitational correspondence, is not less reliable than today's scientific language. It is a pointing and a probing rather than a definitive statement.

Remember, artistic expressions are more easily

understood in love. Open your ears to the subtleties of communication. The bread I baked for my husband today was not my way of merely meeting his need for nourishment; I could have given him a hot dog bun on a paper plate. My baking for him says, you're worth the extra time this takes, you work hard for us—"Happy Friday." I'm also saying, I care that you have healthful, whole wheat nourishment. All these meanings were baked into my bread. I have found that creating allows for a wealth of communication.

Bridging this gap between communication and understanding will demand a lot of us. We need to put aside pride to become willing learners, and we need to exercise patience both as viewer/listeners and as creators, explaining our modes of expression. There is a problem when one looks at modern art and walks away with one question: "Who is the foolish one, myself or the artist?" Pride has become the shield of an artist's vulnerability (and it is a vulnerable thing to lay your work before strangers) and has said to the viewer, "You are too ignorant to understand the depths of white on white or the richness of a blank canvas with a diagonal slash mark." The result: A prideful response that says, "I don't care about you or your crazy art!!"

With so many barriers, one might be tempted to avoid the arts altogether. There is no neutral ground. The question is not: "Should Christians be involved in the arts?" Rather, ask, "Are the arts we produce a vehicle of praise or an expression of human vanity?"[11]

There is not a Christian style that everyone from all time periods should work within. In order to honor the Lord, a contemporary musician need not write in the style of Bach. It is true, however, that there are important considerations that affect a Christian style. If this is not happening, it is because there a certain dichotomy between faith and practice is being lived out.

This challenge is a difficult one for a Christian artist and supporters of the arts (the body of Christ). It is not easy to stand before the Lord and watch the refining fires touch your work. What is needed is reforming reconciliation which will happen in the power of the Holy Spirit. "Holy spirited buildings culturally will be content with beginning at a lesser stage of structural differentiation than the dominant secular phase, so that its specializing integrated service can be developed obediently rather than be caught up in reforming peripheral matters of what is set up secularly."[12]

Leonardo Da Vinci was a better artist for doing anatomical studies and learning structural laws from which to base his style of artistry. We also will be more God-honoring in the arts if we strive to learn how His truths of our redemption, our present struggle, and our assured victory affect our world and affect our aesthetic eye.

Remember, it is His concern, His struggle; therefore, it is ours.

Notes

1. Franky Schaeffer, *Addicted to Mediocrity* (Westchester, IL: Cornerstone Books of Good News, 1981), pp. 62-107.
2. Calvin Seerveld, "The Relation of Arts to the Presentation of Truth" in *Truth and Reality*, Festschrift for H.G. Stoker (Braamfontein: DeJong, 1971), p. 169.
3. *Famous Modern Artists: From Cezanne to Pop Art* (New York: Platt and Munk, 1971), p. 70.
4. William Blake, *The Four Zoas* (ix:855) as quoted in *A Blake Dictionary: The Ideas and Symbols of William Blake* by S. Foster Damon (Providence, RI: Brown University Press, 1965), p. XI.
5. Zuidervaart, Lambert P, *Kant's Critique of Beauty and Taste: Explorations Into Philosophical Aesthetics* (Toronto: Institute for Christian Studies, 1977), p. 32.
6. Calvin Seerveld, *Notes for Aesthetic Life and Artistic Task*, (Wedge Publishing Foundation, 1979), p. 9.
7. Stuart Davis, "How to Construct a Modern Easel Painting" a lecture delivered by Davis at the New School for Social Research, December 17, 1941, as quoted in "Stuart Davis: Pragmatist of American Modernism" by Diane Kelder in *Art Journal*, Fall 1979, XXX IX/1, p.29.
8. Marion Greenwood, quoted in "City and Country in the 1930s: A Study of New Deal Murals in New York" by Marlene Park in *Art Journal*, Fall 1979, XXXIX, 1, p. 44.
9. Calvin Seerveld, "Relating Christianity to the Arts," *Christianity Today*, November 1980, p. 48.
10. H.R. Rookmaaker, *The Creative Gift* (Westchester, IL: Cornerstone Books, 1981), p. 26.
11. Calvin Seerveld, "Relating Christianity to the Arts," p. 48.
12. Calvin Seerveld, *Philosophy in a New Key* (Toronto: Course Notes to Institute for Christian Studies seminar, January 1976), p. 2.

Annotated Bibliography

Rookmaaker, H.R., *The Creative Gift*, Westchester, IL: Cornerstone Books, 1981.

  The late H.R. Rookmaaker wrote this collection of essays which is said to be his "last major statement" on the arts. This three part collection divides itself into the headings: Being Christian in a Broken World, Freedom within a Framework, and Creative Sharing of the Gospel. Rookmaaker himself was a professor of Art History at the Free University of Amsterdam, The Netherlands, until his death in 1977. He has certainly left his mark on Christian thinking.

Rookmaaker, H.R., *Art Needs No Justification*, Downers Grove, IL: InterVarsity Press, 1978.

  Written by H.R. Rookmaaker, yet left uncompiled until after his death, this booklet purposes to encourage *all* Christians who desire to see their God-given talents used to the glory of God, the Giver. A historical background supports a critique of present work, and a striving for a Christian framework for future endeavors. This is short, readable and insightful.

Ryken, Leland, ed., *The Christian Imagination*, Grand Rapids, MI: Baker Book House, 1981.

  This is a collection of 32 essays dealing with such topics as: A philosophy of the arts, literature, the visual arts, and music. Contribution authors are many of the most recognized and respected Christian scholars in their fields. It is a good overview of Christian thinking expressed in a variety of styles. The editor, Leland Ryken, is a professor of English at Wheaton College.

Seerveld, Calvin, *Rainbows for the Fallen World*, Toronto: Tuppence Press, 1980.

  Written by a man often quoted by others in his field, this book deals with pursuing an understanding of God's calling on our aesthetic values. To read Seerveld's book is to strive with him to appreciate and respond to this calling. We highly recommend this reading as very important in developing a God honoring pursuit of Christianity and the Arts. Seerveld's work, *A Christian Critique of Art and Literature* (Wedge) is also a good source.

Zuidervaart, Lambert, *Kant's Critique of Beauty and Taste: Explorations into a Philosophical Aesthetics*, Toronto: Institute for Christian Studies, 1977.

This is Lambert Paul Zuidervaart's Thesis submitted for a Masters Degree in Philosophy and Aesthetics at the Free University. Although not necessarily written for easy readability, there are nevertheless many nuggets of truth to be considered. Zuidervaart explores the content and implications of Kant's critiques which have so strongly influenced the philosophers and aestheticians from the late 1700s to present. Zuidervaart now teaches at King's College in Edmonton, Alberta.

Chapter 7

"The Age of Science and Technology" Comes of Age?

What Am I Getting Into?

When I decided to enter college to study chemical engineering, I thought I'd already learned my lessons on religion well. I knew that a Christian's point of view differed in significant ways from that of the nonbeliever:

—Christians view humanity as the result of God's creative process, as well as the focus of His desire for responsive children;

—Christians place ultimate faith in God and His faithfulness, not in the creaturely achievements of humanity—no matter how these achievements appeared to solve problems;

—and Christians desire to pursue knowledge both as an attempt to fulfill the universal demand for human stewardship of the creation, and to provide insight into the proper relationship with the Creator.

Older members of the church told me it would be an error to blunt or ignore these distinctions.

Warnings came in from friends who have entered graduate school at State University: "You've got to be careful not to get caught by the absence of thorough, analytic thinking." Such absence would produce confusion, blurred distinctions, and an only partly Christian perspective. They warned me against attractive philosophies that had been "baptized," producing "Christian-something-ism" as a new hybrid. If a current system of philosophy is combined with Christianity, the Christian faith always suffers dilution. If the presuppositions of the philosophy

110

are ignored, the Christian contrast fades away. Watch out for the tendency to ignore the presuppositions in favor of the superficial similarities, they said. Eclecticism always produces unhealthy pluralism!

I also knew better than to take the route of "escapism."

> *You can imagine how excited I was when I was invited to attend a lecture by a Professor teaching Technology and Public Policy. The minister who invited me said he knew the Professor would bring his Christian faith and his research together in a way that would prove helpful to those of us at the threshold of our careers.*
>
> *The minister was only partially accurate . . . The professor did share how he had come to believe that Jesus Christ was his personal savior, and some ways in which his faith had grown. Then came a time for questions: When asked, "How does your faith in Jesus influence your work in nuclear research?" the Professor answered, "I don't think about those things; the end is near and the Lord is coming back to destroy the earth. All that we do now will be burned up anyway!"*

If our concept of science ignores God's love for the *cosmos* (in John 3:16 the Greek word for creation is used) then the redemptive touch of the Body of Christ upon culture (institutions, arts, education, economics, ecology, etc.) does not exist. All that is left is to pronounce a final curse and leave the good but perverted-by-sin creation to perish. Such a gross reduction is thoroughly anti-Christian.

How did we get to the place where our concept of God and our appreciation of science are so widely separated? In writing of humanity in our time, a time frequently summarized by the phrase "man's conquest of nature," C.S. Lewis writes:

> The serious magical endeavour and the serious scientific endeavour are twins: one was sickly and died and the other throve. But they are twins. They were born of the same impulse. I allow that some (certainly not all) of the early scientists were actuated by a pure love of knowledge. But if we consider the temper of that age as a whole we can discern the impulse of which I speak. There is something which unites magic and applied science while separating both from the "wisdom" of earlier ages. For the wise men

of old the cardinal problem had been how to conform the soul to reality, and the solution had been knowledge, self-discipline and virtue. For magic and applied science alike the problem is how to subdue reality to the wishes of men: the solution is a technique; and both, in the practice of this technique, are ready to do things hitherto regarded as disgusting and impious—such as digging up and mutilating the dead . . . It might be going too far to say that the modern scientific movement was tainted from its birth: but I think it would be true to say that it was born in an unhealthy neighbourhood and at an inauspicious hour. Its triumph may have been too rapid and purchased at too high a price: reconsideration, something like repentance, may be required.[1]

Almost thirty years after Lewis spoke his words, we are saturated with electronic technology: the 1982 *Time* magazine "man of the year" was a computer![2] To raise a question about science's all-encompassing, all-pervasive, all-powerful presence appears to be a form of cultural blasphemy. Yet we must ask: What is the legitimate role of science—servant of our God-ordained task,[3] or deity to be served and worshipped?

For those who wish to take seriously their role as thoughtful and obedient servants in God's vineyard, the question is: How is my life as a Christian to be different regarding science?

No matter what your station in life—student in a school which is not scientifically oriented; chemistry major in a highly regarded technical university; working in a "high-tech" electronics industry; citizen, concerned with how government decisions affect the environment; neighbor or relative to someone needing medical attention—in every facet of life, there are major ways science touches our everyday existence. Gerald Holton, Professor of Physics and Professor of History of Science at Harvard University points out:

> More and more frequently, major decisions that profoundly affect our daily lives have a large scientific or technological content. By a recent estimate nearly half the bills before the U.S. Congress have a substantial science-technology component, some two-thirds of the District of Columbia Circuit Court's case load now involves a review of federal administrative agen-

cies; and more and more of such cases relate to matters on the frontiers of technology.[4]

Science touches the lives of us all. Professor Egbert Schuurman of the Delft and Eindhoven Institutes of Technology, The Netherlands, underscores the magnitude of this situation:

> It has been estimated that perhaps eighty percent of all the scientists and engineers who ever lived are living today. A figure like that makes one realize the exceptional character of our time. A growing number of people have jobs related in one way or another to the development of science and technology. In addition they find themselves surrounded more and more by the products of technology, both on the job and at home. We live in a technological society that is growing all the time in strength and scope and that is spreading across the globe.[5]

We must work to clarify how science should be understood and used in God's creation.

Those who observe the decline of Christian influence (belief) in the face of the overwhelming tide of scientific/ empirical floodwaters present a pessimistic picture of Christianity:

> . . .there is no way around the painful dilemma in which the religious traditions of the world have found themselves trapped over the last two centuries. Every culture that has invested its convictions in a temporal-physical mythology is doomed before the onslaught of the scientific unbeliever . . . Indeed, the sweeping secularization of Western society that has come in the wake of scientific advance can be seen as a product of Christianity's peculiar reliance on a precarious, dogmatic literalism.[6]

The areas of conflict between Science and the Bible are not the issue of this chapter. Those matters are not unimportant; however, the scope of this examination is a general picture of science and the Christian faith. This discussion is more closely related to the laboratory and the classroom than to the church building and Bible study. It should be strongly stated that the source for our understanding of all of reality is the Bible. Also, there is much material on the topic of the tension between the Bible and science which can be studied profitably.[7]

Science/Scientific Method/Scientism

Why is it that every elementary science text has a single (and presumably comprehensive!) definition for science? Frequently these definitions focus on a single "scientific method." Should we settle for a method of gaining empirical data as "the way" of viewing science? Are we to accept an understanding of the universe which limits it to empirical sense-data and presupposes a particular form of "correct thinking"? Actually, definitions of science vary greatly:

> Science: Knowledge of facts, phenomena, laws, and proximate causes, gained and verified by exact observation, organized experiment and correct thinking; also, the sum of universal knowledge (Funk and Wagnall's *New College Standard Dictionary*).

> Science is the investigation of the physical universe and its ways and consists largely of weighing, measuring, and putting things in test tubes. To assume that this kind of investigation can unearth solutions to all man's problems is a form of religious faith whose bankruptcy has only in recent years started to become apparent (Frederick Buechner).[8]

> Knowledge progresses only when it is understood to survive the passing of particular minds or generations. Science, understood as the expanding application of a fixed method of knowing to ever more areas of experience, makes such a claim (Theodore Roszak).[9]

> There is no simple definition which will enable people to determine exactly what is scientific, and what is not. Each definition must be supplemented by detailed explanation, and though there is a core of agreement in the explanations these differ on some important points (A.H. Hobbs).[10]

Another definition now widely circulated through the writings of Thomas Kuhn is: " 'Normal science' means research firmly based upon one or more past scientific achievements, achievements that some particular scientific community acknowledges for a time as supplying the foundation for its further practice."[11] In a lighter, but accurate vein, Frederick Buechner provides a contrast to the straightforward approach taken by others:

> A scientist's views on such subjects as God,

morality, life after death, are apt to be about as enlightening as a theologian's views on the structure of the atom or the cause and cure of the common cold.

The conflict between science and religion, which reached its peak toward the end of the last century, is like the conflict between a podiatrist and a poet. One says that Susie Smith has fallen arches. The other says she walks in beauty like the night. In his own way each is speaking the truth. What is at issue is the kind of truth you're after.[12]

Part of our continuing frustration is that in the presence of this type of diversity of perspective there is an exaggerated view of the role of science. With a commitment frequently referred to as scientism, our culture believes that science can provide answers to all human problems.[13] This clearly makes science a replacement for religion. The prevailing cultural view is that science alone encompasses all knowledge. Down through history religion has often been seen in this way, but now science, and in the exaggerated form of scientism, becomes a religion. H.E. Runner writes: "Basically scientism is modern man's worship, the expression of his apostate religion."[14] As with most "isms" there is a "good" on which it is based—in this case a good prescription from God: humanity called to be the stewards of the creation—but the human desire for absolute freedom takes the good gift and makes it a perversion.

How does science fare according to its own criteria? Science changes—but then what about those scientists who once held with absolute certainty (and sincerity!) to an earlier system, now discarded as unscientific? Jonathan Miller, writing on the history of medicine, demonstrates that people were limited by conceptual models for understanding the functions of internal organs. Pumps, furnaces, sailing vessels, and rotations of the planets all were the models for the system (world-view) of various historical periods. In discussing Franz Anton Mesmer's 1776 work on the influence of the stars and planets on human health, Miller writes:

> . . . Mesmer tried his best to reconcile the occult superstitions of the Renaissance with the scientific principles of the Age of Reason. The English physicist Isaac Newton provided him with a convenient rationale. At the end of his *Principles of Natural Philosophy* Newton had invited his readers to con-

sider the possibility that the universe was pervaded by an Aether, and that this might explain the transmission of light, magnetism, and gravity . . . "Magnetism" was no more irrational, no more scientific, than the orthodox remedies of purging, bloodletting, and cupping. Even at the end of the eighteenth century, so-called conventional medicine was a tissue of contradictions: there were no consistent intellectual standards and no organized body of scientific principles.[15]

How can we be expected to ascribe the fixed values associated with religion, and to commit our lives to faith in a system of belief which continues to fluctuate (to the point of denying the validity of earlier, firmly held truth!) throughout time? As Theodore Roszak writes, "Science is the infidel to all gods in behalf of none."[16] New scientific thought is the ultimate authority which undermines previous "scientific" systems, as well as any other older belief systems.

Certainty

When we consider the attitude of our culture toward science, we become immediately aware of awe and reverence—an almost tangible outworking of our religious commitment. This could happen only where the credibility of anything "scientific" is held to be beyond reproach.

The advertiser who places the model in a white lab coat, the "4 out of 5 doctors" who recommend the product, the unpronounceable ingredient, and the exact "percentage of increased whiteness" are only a few examples of the commercial value in using a "scientific approach."

Is it possible that in our age of seeking for clear authority, easy-to-follow steps of action, and instant results, we invest in the scientific community our hope that they will provide these things? In other areas of cultural expression, the absence of "heroes" has produced a vacuum filled by the "anti-hero" (some of the successful singers in the pop/rock market), or perhaps a yearning for the return of the simple folk hero ("Rocky"). In the arena of science and technology, many remain convinced that there are "easy solutions," if only the reins of decision making would be turned over to a scientific oligarchy.

Many social commentators see in increased technology an indication of our culture's submission to this type of rule.

The term most frequently used to describe this arrangement is technocracy. It is defined as:

> . . . that society in which those who govern justify themselves by appeal to technical experts who, in turn, justify themselves by appeal to scientific forms of knowledge. And beyond the authority of science, there is no appeal.[17]

In line with this definition, Roszak analyzes our culture as a product of subliminal manipulation:

> The distinctive feature of the regime of experts lies in the fact that, while possessing ample power to coerce, it prefers to charm conformity from us by exploiting our deep-seated commitment to the scientific worldview and by manipulating the securities and creature comforts of the industrial affluence which science has given us.[18]

In illustrating his contentions, Roszak uses the experience (he labels it "technician-paternalism") of the British National Health Service. Anticipating a future of professional control, the Service could (according to a BBC-TV documentary study) look forward to: certifying normalcy, administering a program of voluntary euthanasia, enforcing compulsory contraception, and evaluating genetic qualities of prospective parents.[19] While this may seem overly pessimistic, even as a possibility, this form of technocracy should give no pause when we are asked to place our future in the hands of technocrats.

Professor Schuurman presents a similar critique of technocrats as they apply their formulae to all the areas of life:

> Today's problems, they say, are the problems of a technology in its infancy; they can be solved by exploiting more fully the possibilities of technology. The method of technology should be extended to other areas such as economics and politics. What is good for technology is good for all culture.[20]

The common rationale given for this perspective is that the scientific enterprise affords a certainty—absolute accuracy in measurable terms—which no other system offers. Science has long rejected this appraisal of itself at the professional, philosophic level, but has encouraged this basis of instruction at the introductory classroom level. R.C. Jeffrey writes in *Philosophy of Science*, ". . . I shall suggest that the activity proper to the scientist is the assignment of pro-babilities."[21] This comment occurs in the context of an on-going discussion of the role of scientists in culture: Does the scientist make decisions on the "rightness" of hypotheses or is his role one of "supplier of probabilities" for different (even conflicting!) hypotheses—the decisions to be made by govern-mental, societal agency people?[22]

The elevation or "over-evaluation" of the recommenda-tions made by those involved in science invests the scientist with a certain objectivity. The implicit feeling is that since decisions must be made by someone who is objective and in-formed, the scientist should make them. Who is better than one trained to be objective?

Roszak approaches this conclusion from a similar starting point—"reliable knowledge," as he terms it:

> . . . what is "reliable knowledge"? How do we know it when we see it? The answer is: reliable knowledge is knowledge that is scientifically sound, since science is that to which modern man refers for the definitive explication of reality. And what in turn is it that characterizes scientific knowledge? The answer is: objectivity. Scientific knowledge is not just a feeling or speculation or subjective ruminating. It is a verifiable description of reality that exists indepen-dent of any purely personal considerations. It is true . . . real . . . dependable . . . It works. And that at last is how we define an expert: he is one who really knows what is what, because he cultivates an objective con-sciousness . . . The study of man in his social, political, economic, psychological, historical aspects—all this too must become objective: rigorously, painstakingly objective. At every level of human experience, would-be scientists come forward to endorse the myth of objective consciousness, thus certifying themselves as experts. And because they know and we do not, we yield to their guidance.[23]

Underlining the "reliable and objective" nature of this knowledge brings our attention to the question of neutrality.

Objectivity/Value Free/Neutrality

While holding to the hope of progress toward the ideal of scientific objectivity, Richard Rudner writes:

. . . clearly the scientist as scientist does make value judgements. For since no scientific hypothesis is ever completely verified, in accepting a hypothesis the scientist must make the decision that the evidence is *sufficiently* strong or that the probability is *sufficiently* high to warrant acceptance of the hypothesis.[24]

Those who have been most supportive of the concept of the neutrality of science say that "We have arrived!" is a misrepresentation of scientific fact.

It is also the case that when science is taught at the introductory level, it is frequently presumed that the history of science has proceeded in a straight line (or at least in a well-ordered "stair-step" of hypothesis built upon hypothesis confirmed, etc.). Again, this is not supported by the evidence. Theodore Roszak summarizes the argument from Thomas Kuhn's *The Structure of Scientific Revolutions*:

> His contention comes close to suggesting that the progressive accumulation of "truth" in the scientific community is something of an illusion, created by the fact that each generation of scientists rewrites its textbooks in such a way as to select from the past what is still considered valid and to suppress the multitude of errors and false starts that are also a part of the history of science.[25]

In an article well supported both by examples from contemporary textbooks and illustrations from the history of specific scientific disciplines, Stephen G. Brush challenges the traditionalists in science education:

> My point is that, if science teachers want to use the history of science, and if they want to obtain their information and interpretations from contemporary writings by historians rather than from the myths and anecdotes handed down from one generation of textbook writers to the next, they cannot avoid being influenced by the kind of skepticism about objectivity which is now so widespread . . . Once it has been pointed out that in Galileo's statement, "I have discovered by experiment some properties of (motion)," the words "by experiment" were added in an English translation and do not appear in the original Italian version, it is hard to maintain the traditional faith in Galileo's empiricism.[26]

While emphasizing the practical nature of the student-teacher-classroom relationships, this important article also asks penetrating philosophical questions:

> Are the standards of objective scientific method worth preserving, even as ideals that are rarely attained in practice? Or do we distort our understanding of the nature of science by paying lip service to such standards?[27]

It is generally held to be sacrosanct that science is an objectively true approach to the highest form of knowledge: empirical sense data. What if the premise of this argument is called into question? How is one to continue if the force thought to be holding together the cosmos *isn't*?

Even Brush puts forward the possibility of accepting the functional use of "fictionalized" history of science in order to illustrate one's pronouncements on the scientific method. This suggestion obviously plunges us even deeper into the quicksand of religious substitution. It is a non-solution, a pretense.

Even after having heard the historical and methodological questions, many fiercely defend objectivity as the organizing principle for science. Christians ought not to be surprised by this seeming incongruity. The issue is one of authority and freedom. A reading of Romans 1:18-32 confirms the universal human response to God's authority: rebellion. Even Roszak writes:

> The scientific mind begins in the spirit of the Cartesian zero, with the doubting away of all inherited knowledge in favor of an entirely new method of knowing, which whether it proceeds on rationalist or empirical lines, purports to begin from scratch, free from all homage to authority.[28]

Within the secular philosophical arena the challenge to objectivity has been withstood by the strength of science and technology. Again, Roszak presents the argument forcefully:

> . . . Michael Polanyi has argued [*Personal Knowledge: Towards a Post-Critical Philosophy*, The University of Chicago Press, 1959] there is no such thing as objectivity, even in the physical sciences. Certainly his critique is a formidable challenge to scientific orthodoxy . . . [But] Science, under the technocracy, has become a total culture dominating the lives of millions for whom discussions of the theory of knowledge are so much foreign language. Yet objec-

tivity, whatever its epistemological status, has become the commanding life style of our society: the one most authoritative way of regarding the self, others, and the whole of our enveloping reality.[29]

What Am I To Do?

—Having followed the line of argument which identifies the inadequacies and inappropriate presuppositions of much of the contemporary scientific enterprise, what is the Christian student to do?

—Wishing to avoid subjectivism in the aftermath of rejecting the determinism of scientism, how is the believer to see God's hand at work in the creation . . . even through secondary causes?

—Aware of the religious rootedness—now lost—of much of the history of the physical sciences, is it possible to again appreciate the legitimate role of science in gaining insight into the means God uses to uphold the world?

Perhaps you have been thinking along these lines, or you may have other lingering doubts which reflect your concern to respond as a Christian to science. Whatever the particulars may be, the heading of this section, "What am I to do?," most likely captures the thrust.

There are those who have begun to address this issue, and have provided some ideas for a helpful place to begin.

Contextually, it is important to note that God calls none of us to stand alone, isolated from brothers and sisters who comprise the Body of Christ. Pray for relationships with others who have similar concerns who will join in praying, studying, offering evaluations of class assignments, and encouraging one another. There are organized groups who are attempting to follow the concept of the Lordship of Jesus Christ into the academic and professional situations of science and technology. (See Annotated Bibliography)

Dr. Robert E. Vander Vennen has addressed this question and suggests that believing scientists (no less than any who place their allegiance in the Christian faith) must work to identify a "Christian Mind" (as Harry Blamires has put it). Included is a careful and accurate use of language. While using commonly accepted terms, the Christian as scientist will see God's sustaining hand in much of what science views as a law-prescribed closed system. (cf. Ps. 147:15-18, Rom. 11:36, Mt. 5:45)[30] The work for the serious person is clearly multiplied:

to learn the content of scientific discipline; to study the philosophic presuppositions; to review these presuppositions in light of God's revealed Truth; and to lovingly bring clarity and critique to discussion with others.

One final contribution to this discussion comes from Professor Arie Leegwater. In order to contextualize the work of science, the organizing principle should be a correct view of creation:

> . . . I wish to appeal to the Biblical view of creation, that is, to creation which reveals God's normative good order and will for our lives from the beginning.
>
> This emphasis on creation is not an extra factor, one among many, but is rather an expression of our human condition. Man stands in Covenant with God and responds in one way or another to God's revelation in creation . . . We indeed live in a God-ordered world. That revelation is as bright as the sun, as near to us as the falling rain, and as down-to-earth as the farmer's agricultural practices mentioned in Isaiah 28:23-29.
>
> . . . The heart of the scientific enterprise is first of all not science and its (tentative) results, but rather the Truth (the Revelation) by which science is to be practiced. That Truth cannot be objectified, pointed to, or put down on paper. Rather it is the source of renewal and the horizon of our life in all its multiplicity of actions.[31]

The crucial need is for a balanced view of science (properly rooted in and guided by God's Truth) as a tool for human stewardship. One significant danger among followers of our Lord is to locate the problems of humanity in science. As Schuurman writes:

> There is a real danger that science and technology *as such* will be blamed for our present dilemma. In many quarters, in fact, people have already come to this conclusion. But then the nature of our crisis has been woefully misunderstood. It is not science or technology but *man* that bears the blame. Western man has chosen to accept this world and himself as his first and last point of reference. He has gradually closed his eyes to any transcendent reality. The purpose of history and the meaning of life have been restricted to this world; they have been made imma-

nent. And man, no longer open to God, is now thrown
back on a purely this-worldly reality.[32]

Only with an appreciation for our role as creatures and
developers of the creation, can we find the dimensions of joy
and hope which God has built into the created order.[33]

Illustrating how the creation careens out of control when
the Creator is denied, Professor Schuurman presents the
following analysis of fallen humanity's desire for autonomy
and the effects on the eco-structure:

> The dominant view in modern technology, therefore,
> is that man is in a position to command the world as
> he wishes. With technology as his tool, man sets out
> to create a world in which he alone is lord and
> master. He is motivated and stimulated to do this
> because of his need to safeguard his autonomous
> position, so that he may continue to enjoy and con-
> sume the fruits of his own labor . . .
>
> In so doing, man reduces reality to one of its
> aspects. Reality, however, will not tolerate such
> reduction because it consists of a diversity of aspects.
> Everything in reality exists in a coherence of meaning
> given with creation itself; man cannot reject this
> coherence without suffering the consequences . . .
> The nature we control and dominate threatens to
> turn on us. Destroyed and polluted, it has become a
> definite threat to the survival of mankind. The
> religious faith in progress has combined with
> technological progress itself to bring mankind to a
> critical stage.
> . . . Sovereign and autonomous man has become con-
> scious of his unique position in creation; at the same
> time he has perverted this position because he fails to
> observe the normative restrictions it entails. Thus he
> chooses to abuse nature rather than manage it ac-
> cording to his original mandate. The normative rela-
> tionship between technology and nature is broken.
> Man uses technology so that nature is exhausted
> prematurely, while everything that does not fit into
> the scheme of technological control is wiped out.
> Instead of promoting harmony between
> technology and nature and thereby unfolding nature
> according to its meaning, man interferes in nature in
> such a way that he devastates it.

> ... Man has developed a technology that threatens his
> survival; he has become the victim of technology in-
> stead of its master.[34]

Technology has become the arena for head-to-head confron-
tations between the various scientific/religious presuppositions of our day. Technology is not the enemy, but it does contain the seeds for its own destruction through its absolutizing
of the scientific-technological method as the only basis for
knowledge. Again, Professor Schuurman sets the material in
balance:

> Although no one can supply the full meaning of
> technology, we can state it in part. Technology will be
> able to alleviate the fate forced on man "by nature."
> It will offer greater opportunities for living: reducing
> the physical burdens and strains inherent in labour,
> diminishing the drudgery of routine duties, averting
> natural catastrophies, conquering diseases, supply-
> ing homes and food, augmenting social security, ex-
> panding possibilities for communications, increasing
> information and responsibility, advancing material
> welfare in harmony with spiritual well-being, and
> helping unfold the abundance of individual qualities
> in people. Moreover, in science and in its own field,
> technology will develop new possibilities for pro-
> moting a variegated disclosure of society. Technology
> will also make possible labour that is meaningful as
> well as productive; it will provide room for work that
> is marked by creativity, service, love, and care. It will
> also provide room for leisure and reflection.
>
> This picture of technology, however, is not how it
> actually functions today. Inspired by wrong motives,
> modern technology has been made into a threat to
> nature, culture and man; whereas the right motive
> would lead technology to contribute to the unfolding
> of nature and to the enrichment and deepening of
> culture and human life.[35]

Schuurman provides one specific illustration:

> The case of the computer is quite similar. A sober
> analysis indicates that the computer works fast and
> accurately and that its results will never go beyond
> the programmed instructions. Yet people's fear of
> growing more dependent on the computer remains
> real because the computer operates independently of

man himself, because its results contain a limited element of surprise, and because the user is not
necessarily the programmer. Moreover since the user
changes again and again, he cannot know by what set
of criteria the computer works; he is forced to surrender himself in trust to the dictates of the computer. This problem will be aggravated when the self-
adapting and self-reproductive machines, predicted
by computer specialists, are introduced in the
future.[36]

In the face of this pressure, Schuurman proposes a more adequate emphasis on the philosophy of technology. Through the
study of the relationship of science and technology to the rest
of the created order, the questions which arise could be dealt
with in their appropriate order. Without some grasp of the
philosophy of technology—by those who are the im-
plementers as well as the designers of the technology—every
question becomes one of technique, never presuppositions!
When properly approached, the questions of presuppositions,
values, ethics, and priorities would preceed technical solutions.

Another illustration of the misuse of the scien-
tific/technological aspects of our society is offered by Jeremy
Rifkin in his widely discussed book, *Algeny*:

What the "record" shows is nearly a century of
fudging and finagling by scientists attempting to
force various fossil morsels and fragments to conform with Darwin's notions, all to no avail. Today the
millions of fossils stand as very visible, ever-present
reminders of the paltriness of the arguments and the
overall shabbiness of the theory that marches under
the banner of evolution.[37]

Rifkin moves to a picture of the changes in modern biology:

The fact of the matter is, biology is being totally
revamped along engineering lines . . .

Perhaps the best way to express the extent to
which engineering has been able to recast the field of
biology in its own image is to take a look at the word
"performance." Engineers use this word to refer to
the activity of machines. Biologists in contrast have
traditionally relied on the word "behavior" when
referring to the activity of living organisms . . .
scholars go on to say that the term "performance" is

being relied on increasingly as biologists begin to redefine living organisms in terms of relative efficiencies. Clearly the engineering mentality has taken hold within biology . . .[38]

These illustrations are only suggestive. In every discipline of science, in every vocation within our scientific-technological society, we are confronted with the results of our misguided-by-sin treatment of science. Whether in science education, scientific research, technological business, military, or environmental application, we are faced with a significant challenge.

It is with the goal of recapturing all facets of the kingdom for the rightful King that we are to enter obediently into the sphere to which we have been sent. If that sphere is science, then we are to plant the flag of His Lordship firmly upon this part of His good creation. Hard work? Yes, but the victory is assured.

Notes

1. Lewis, C.S., *The Abolition of Man* (New York: The MacMillan Co., 1947), pp. 87-89. For additional historical perspective see:

   Brooks, Richard S., *The Interplay Between Science and Religion in England, 1640-1720: A Bibliographic and Historiographic Guide* (Evanston, IL: Garrett-Evangelical Theological Seminar Library, 1975).

   Burtt, Edwin Arthur, *The Metaphysical Foundations of Modern Physical Science* (Garden City, NJ: Doubleday, 1952).

   Hooykaas, R., *Religion and the Rise of Science* (Grand Rapids, MI: William B. Eerdmans,1972).

   Klaaren, Eugene M., *Religious Origins of Modern Science* (Grand Rapids, MI: William B. Eerdmans, 1977).

   Noll, Mark, "Who Sets the Stage for Understanding Scripture?", *Christianity Today*, May 23, 1980, Vol. XXIV, No. 16, pp. 618-622.

2. *Time*, January 3, 1983, Vol. 121, No. 1.

3. For a further explanation of this concept see, Chapter 1, Bradshaw Frey, *et. al.*, *All of Life Redeemed* (Jordan Station, Ontario, Canada: Paideia Press, 1983).

4. Holton, Gerald, *The Chronicle of Higher Education*, May 18, 1981, quoted in *A Christian Manifesto*, Francis A. Schaeffer (Westchester, IL: Crossway Books, 1982), pp. 80-81.

5. Schuurman, Egbert, *Reflections on the Technological Society* (Toronto: Wedge Publishing Foundation, 1977), p. 1.

6. Roszak, Theodore, *The Making of a Counter Culture* (New York: Anchor Books, 1969), pp. 211, 212. This author is cited as a critic of our present cultural milieu. He is an advocate of the counterculture approach popularized in the late 1960's and the early 1970's. Egbert Schuurman (*Reflections*, pages 49-55) provides some analysis of Roszak's work:

> The distinguishing feature of the counterculture, therefore, is that it offered a limited human scale, that was varied even in its social forms, rather than monotonously identical at every level. It stressed the organic above the mechanical, simplicity and frugality above abundance and delightful labour above production-oriented labour.
>
> Thus countercultural advocates called attention to many important issues often neglected in the past. Much of their analysis of the technological-scientific culture was correct, especially their critical observations concerning the structure of science and their emphasis on the religious backgrounds of the issues they raised.
>
> However, when the apologists of the counterculture reacted against the adulation of science and technology, they reduced them to a mere requirement for the survival of mankind. Since they did not recognize a cultural mandate, they have been unable to shape an alternative direction for the present culture or even to deflect its current direction. In effect, the ideas they introduced into public discussions could only sponge on a culture that is internally torn and segmented . . .
>
> When Christians, at least those who hold a dualistic view of life, associate themselves with this dominant persuasion [a passion for perfection through secularized science], Roszak is correct in accusing them of complicity in the realization of our science-infused culture. However, positivists and

Marxists are often correct as well in charging Christians with opposing science and technology. They reach this conclusion because they frequently observe Christians who oppose the development of science and technology as a result of their failure to integrate a responsible attitude towards it with their dependence on a transcendent reality. Such Christians neglect the fact that the Christian faith embraces values pertaining to created reality . . .

Roszak rejects the prevailing trend of our culture. So do I. But unlike him, I would like to defend an alternative approach in which a transcendental orientation includes responsibility for technological-scientific development.

7. Particular helps include:

    Bube, Richard H., *The Human Quest: A new look at science and the Christian faith* (Waco, TX: Word Books, 1971).

    Hart, Hendrik and James H. Olthuis, "Theses on Science," monograph distributed by The Association for the Advancement of Christian Scholarship, 229 College Street, Toronto, Canada M5T 1R4.

    Olthuis, James H., "The Word of God and Science," monograph distributed by The Association for the Advancement of Christian Scholarship, 229 College Street, Toronto, Canada M5T 1R4.

8. Buechner, Frederick, *Wishful Thinking* (New York: Harper & Row, 1973), p. 86.

9. Roszak, *Culture*, p. 214.

10. Hobbs, A.H., *Social Problems and Scientism* (Harrisburg, PA: Stackpole, 1953), p. 5.

11. Kuhn, Thomas S., *The Structure of Scientific Revolutions* (Chicago: The University of Chicago Press, 1962 & 1970), p. 10. As Kuhn illustrates through his use of paradigms, those who learn from the same conceptual models tend not to disagree over fundamentals.

12. Buechner, *Wishful Thinking*, p. 86. Also, cf. Schuurman, *Reflections*, pp. 3-5, "technocrats—also known as ideologists of planning."

13. Cf. Hobbs, p. 17, note 6.

14. Runner, H.E., *The Relation of the Bible to Learning* (Toronto: Wedge, 1970), from excerpted portion pp. 95-123.

15. Miller, Jonathan, *The Body in Question* (New York: Vin-

tage Books, 1978), pp. 73-76.

16. Roszak, *Culture*, p. 211.
17. Roszak, *Culture*, p. 8.
18. Roszak, *Culture*, p. 9.
19. Roszak, *Culture*, pp. 19-21.
20. Schuurman, *Reflections*, pp. 1,2.
21. Jeffrey, Richard C., "Valuation and Acceptance of Scientific Hypotheses," *Philosophy of Science*, Vol. 23, No. 3, July, 1956 (Williams & Wilkins, Baltimore, MD), p. 237.
22. Schuurman, *Reflections*, pp. 6,7. There are those, Schuurman calls them "revolutionary utopians, or critical futurologists," who "are opposed to a rigid, highly deterministic future under the leadership of a technocratic elite." But, as he demonstrates, there is little Christian or biblical underpinning, thus no suitable replacement of central values is possible. One illustration of this is the revolutionary dialectic of Marxist and neo-Marxist countries.
23. Roszak, *Culture*, pp. 208, 209.
24. Rudner, Richard, "No Science Can Be Value-Free," *Philosophy of Science*, Vol. 20, No. 1, January, 1953 (The Williams & Wilkins Co., Baltimore, MD), p. 2.
25. Roszak, *Culture*, p. 213.
26. Brush, Steven G., "Should the History of Science Be Rated X?", *Science*, Vol. 183, No. 4130, March 22, 1974 (American Association for the Advancement of Science, Washington, DC), p. 1170.
27. Brush, "Rated X", p. 1170.
28. Roszak, *Culture*, p. 213.
29. Roszak, *Culture*, pp. 215, 216.
30. Vander Vennen, Robert, "Is Scientific Research Value-Free?" *Journal of the American Scientific Affiliation*, 27 (September, 1977), pp. 107-111.
31. Leegwater, Arie, "Creation: Does It Matter?", *Life Is Religion*, Henry Vander Goot, ed., (St. Catharines, Ontario: Paideia Press, 1981), pp. 259, 260.
32. Schuurman, *Reflections*, p. 15.
33. Frey, *et. al.*, *Life Redeemed*, Chapters 1, 2, plus references for the development of this idea.
34. Schuurman, *Reflections*, pp. 32-35.
35. Schuurman, *Reflections*, pp. 59-60.
36. Schuurman, *Reflections*, p. 43.
37. Rifkin, Jeremy, *Algeny* (New York: The Viking Press, 1983), p. 125. For a less positive view of Rifkin's efforts (in

evaluating Darwin/evolution, "Rifkin gets quite mystical
at times . . .") see "Debunking Darwin," Niles Eldredge,
Physchology Today, June, 1983, pp. 12-13. Eldredge is not
any more affirming of Rifkin's work of predicting the
future aspects of the biotechnological revolution—criticizing his absence of content on genetic
engineering and energy use. [It seems fair to point out,
however, that Rifkin has been involved in authoring other
works which have dealt exclusively with these issues. His
present effort seems directed at more of the philosophical
background and leaves the technical matters for these
other books.]
38. Rifkin, *Algeny*, p. 202.

Annotated Bibliography

Barcus, Nancy B., *Developing a Christian Mind*, Downers
    Grove, IL: InterVarsity Press, 1977.
    Setting out with the hope that "the keen-minded reader
    will find an outlook here that will make believing and
    thinking a compatible and joyful pair," the author
    surveys science, nature, and humanism. This survey
    produces both reflection and challenge to the
    thoughtful, and encouragement for the confused. The
    chapter "Meaning and the Shattered Box: Science," pro-
    vides an overview of the forces producing our present
    atmosphere of scientific omnipotence; it suggests an ap-
    proach to dialogue and asks penetrating questions
    about the present scientific framework.
Burrt, Edwin Arthur, *The Metaphysical Foundations of
    Modern Science*, Garden City, NY: Doubleday Anchor
    Books, 1952.
    Among the several books tracing the influences of con-
    cepts of "ultimate reality" and the causal efficacy of the
    empirical and sensory, this work does more than re-
    count the details of Copernicus, Kepler, Galileo, Gilbert,
    Boyle, and Newton. The author identifies presupposi-
    tions and the importance of the role of the philosophy of
    science as it develops through the centuries. Questions
    of empiricism, mechanism, and a proper understanding
    of the concept of *a priori*, focus on the problem of reduc-
    tionism.
Jaeves, Malcolm A., *The Scientific Enterprise and Christian
    Faith*, Downers Grove, IL: InterVarsity Press, 1969.

This work reflects the interaction of thirty-six scientists from ten countries at the International Conference of Science and Faith at Oxford, July, 1965. History and philosophy of science are summarized, and discussion is of points of concern: cosmology, evolution, and origin of life.

Kuhn, Thomas S., *The Structure of Scientific Revolutions*, Chicago: The University of Chicago Press, 1962, 1970.

Discussing movement from questions concerning objectivity and disjuncture to the concept of paradigms, the author emphasizes the importance of the history of science. It is only as the continuing thread of subsequent "revolutions" is pursued that we can see the role of earlier "revolutions." Commentary on the historical function of Boyle: "Other revolutions, including the one that centers around Lavoisier, were required to give the concept (defining element in relation to chemical manipulation and chemical theory) its modern form and function. But Boyle provides a typical example both of the process involved at each of these stages and of what happens to that process when existing knowledge is embodied in a textbook. More than any other single aspect of science, that pedagogic form has determined our image of the nature of science and of the role of discovery and invention in its advance" (p. 143).

Lakatos, Imre and Alan Musgrave (eds.), *Criticism and the Growth of Knowledge*, Cambridge: Cambridge University Press, 1970.

This work is the accumulation of papers from the International Colloquium in the Philosophy of Science, London, 1965. Of particular interest is the paper "Logic of Discovery or Psychology of Research" by Thomas S. Kuhn. In this paper he evaluates his own concept of how science grows in relation to the work of Sir Karl Popper.

Rifkin, Jeremy, *Algeny*, New York: The Viking Press, 1983.

In evaluating the future of biotechnology, the author analyzes Darwinism. Seeing it as a reflection of its cultural milieu, he presents a case for replacing the evolutionary model with a new one based in part on new technology, energy sources, and humanity's continuing desire to attain control.

Roszak, Theodore, *The Making of a Counter Culture*, Garden City, NY: Doubleday Anchor Books, 1969.

Surviving the decade and a half since its publication,

this work provides the basis for a reaction to the tight
control of the scientific/technological perspective.
Growing out of the inquiries of the "anti-establishment"
era, the questioning of basic commitment to "objective
consciousness" and "technology" on the part of our
culture are still very valuable.

Schuurman, Egbert, *Reflections on the Technological Society*,
Toronto: Wedge Publishing Foundation, 1977.

A collection of essays (given from 1973-1975), the work
deals with: 1) the tension between technology and
revolution; 2) the spiritual roots of the environmental
crisis; and 3) an evaluation of the relation between
science and culture. The third topic has particular impact on the student of science in our times.

Chapter 8

Give Us This Day Our Daily News

"**F**aster than a speeding bullet. More powerful than a locomotive . . . In a never-ending battle for Truth, Justice, and the American Way." Of course, it's Superman, but this description could be just as true of Clark Kent, "mild-mannered reporter for the *Daily Planet*." When we consider the nature, history and current state of the mass news media, we realize that this institution can leap not only buildings but continents. Faster than a speeding bullet, its television cameras, videotape and microwave transmission bring its audience to the very scene of events, whether street fighting in the Mid-East or moon-walking. If you are a person who prays for international concerns, chances are that you know what to pray about because of some journalist whose vocation it is to pursue that never-ending search for Truth, Justice and the American Way, whether it be in Poland, El Salvador, Afghanistan, or some other far corner of the globe.

When we consider that American radio and television has the largest audience in the world with just under 100% of American households involved, that, in 1977, 3.5 million adults watched daily the ABC, CBS, and NBC evening news programs, 47.3 million people made up the combined reader-ship of three weekly newsmagazines (*Newsweek*, *Time*, and *U.S. News and World Report*), and that just short of 103.5 million adults looked at a daily newspaper that year, we realize the powerful influence the mass news media has on our lives.[1] Our view of the world around us, topics of conversation ("Did you read in the paper last night about . . ."), and to some extent our opinions and attitudes at home, in the market

133

place, and at the polls, are shaped by our understanding of events and life as presented to us by the news media. Journalists determine to a large measure the agenda of discussion, concern, and debate involved in our daily lives. How are Christians to understand "the news" in light of a biblical view of life and society? Let us begin our discussion of this by examining the history and nature of "news telling."

Theories of News Telling

Historically, the role of "the press" in society has been to criticize and oversee the actions and conduct of government. In 1828 an Englishman, Macaulay, coined the phrase "the fourth estate" to describe the press as a fourth participant in the governmental process by informing the people on the formation of government policy. Since it was a watchdog of the government, it was vitally important that the press remain free. This theme, which to this day runs deep in American life, was emphasized by Thomas Jefferson at the beginning of this country: "No government ought to be without censors; and where the press is free, none ever will."[2] Curtis D. MacDougall reemphasized this founding point for journalists today:

> Only a competent and responsible journalism can provide the knowledge and understanding the masses of mankind need in order to maintain government of the people, by the people, for the people.[3]

The constant criticism and surveillance of government by the press, is considered so essential to the successful working of a democracy that the freedom of the press is protected by the First Amendment to the Constitution. This is to preserve the ideals of democracy and guard against any authoritarian governing by the elite.

The importance of this preservation can be traced to the beginnings of mass communication in about 1450. In the authoritarian climate of the early Renaissance, the individual was important only as a member of the community serving the state. Only those in power could know the truth, and they set, changed, and approved what the people knew. The press was considered a servant of the state, obligated to support the royal policy or suffer censorship or punishment. Maintaining government surveillance was obviously not one of its functions. This authoritarian theory of the press was accepted throughout the sixteenth and most of the seventeenth century in Colonial America and Western Europe, and is still found to some extent in all parts of the world.

However, the philosophical climate of the Enlightenment, along with the growth of democracy and capitalism, led to a different understanding of the individual and society and demanded a new concept of the press which became known as the *libertarian* theory. In this theory, the state is no longer paramount and does not have a monopoly on truth. The individual, with the power of Reason, can distinguish between truth and error when conflicting evidence or alternatives are presented. Hence, truth is no longer restricted to a select few in power, but is a matter of individual fulfillment. The search for truth became an inalienable, natural right of rational human creatures who seek to satisfy their own enlightened self-interest. Since the individual is paramount in the society, as each person seeks what is right and good for him or herself, society will naturally benefit since what is good for the individual will be good for the society. What is needed, then, in order for truth to be discovered is a "free marketplace of ideas" where everyone, weak or strong, minority or majority, has a voice. Also, since the individual in society is supreme and delegates or withdraws powers from the government, it is vital that the people know what government is doing. Therefore, in this context, the press becomes the provider of a marketplace of information and serves as a check on the governing process almost wholly free of government influence. David Leroy and Christopher Sterling summarize the role of the press as one feature of a society that strove for the minimal amount of government and that advocated individual freedom:

> Assumptions about the freedom of the press revolved around a notion called "the marketplace of ideas." An unfettered press insured that all ideas would be made public and, more important, once published and debated, the truth would triumph because rational men would discover what was truthful.[4]

In this theory, the freedom guaranteed to the press by the Constitution is essentially a freedom without definition in that there are no requirements that the press be truthful or intelligent, for instance; and there are few laws to protect people from unjust or injurious reports. Further, the concept is based on the assumption that access to information is free to all and that such access is necessary to present contending

viewpoints and offset them against each other so that truth
might be discovered.

By the early twentieth century several changes had oc-
curred in the press, calling for a reevaluation of libertarian
theory. Among these were competition between newspapers,
sensationalism, and a shift from subscriber to advertiser support. In order to increase circulation, newspapers moved
away from slanted or slanderous stories, became more entertaining with comic strips and sports news, for instance, and
published news that was for everyone, using the "lowest common denominator" factor. This movement was encouraged by
the rise of the telegraph wire service which provided the most
recent news to newspapers across the land and representing
people from a variety of faith commitments, political positions
and ethnic backgrounds. "Objective" reporting, then, became
the norm for journalism; objective meaning free from personal bias or ideological slant. Opinion, it was decided,
belonged to the editorial page, while the news columns were
to be composed of "facts." But what are the "facts"? Lester
Markel demonstrates one way in which the presentation of a
news story goes beyond a mere objective reporting of "facts":

> The average reporter collects fifty facts and out of
> the fifty selects twelve as the important ones, leaving
> out thirty-eight. This is the first exercise of judgment.
> Then he decides which of the twelve facts should con-
> stitute the lead or first paragraph of the story; this
> fact gets prime attention because many readers do
> not go beyond the first paragraph. Second exercise of
> judgment. Then the news editor decides whether the
> story shall go on page 1 or page 29; on page 1 it has
> considerable impact, on page 29 it may go unread.
> Third exercise of judgment.[5]

With the twentieth century rise of electronic mass media,
the assumption—which is "necessary" for truth to triumph—that access to publication was free to all, came under
question, along with the concept of objectivity in journalism.
Now, as Siebert, Petterson and Schramm point out:

> Three television, four radio networks, three wire ser-
> vices, shape a large part of the information that goes
> into the American home. In other words, the press, as
> in the old authoritarian days, is falling into the hands
> of a powerful few.[6]

The limiting of the channels of communication made it very

difficult for the press or the mass media to be a free marketplace of ideas, and hence, the assumption undergirding the libertarian theory of the press no longer held. Therefore, those persons who controlled the news channels, the gathering and processing of information, had to accept a new responsibility to society along with assuming protection against government interference. The Commission on Freedom of the Press published the Hutchins Commission Report with the title *A Free and Responsible Press.*[7] The reforms proposed had been suggested by editors and publishers long before the document was published; however, it reveals an important trend. Here is a five point summary of the report.

> 1. The press must provide a truthful, comprehensive, and intelligent account of the day's events in a context which gives them meaning.
> 2. It must be a forum for the exchange of comment and criticism.
> 3. It must project a representative picture of the constituent groups in society.
> 4. It must present and clarify the goals and values of society.
> 5. It must offer full access to the day's intelligence.[8]

Of course these ideas can not be made into laws, since the Constitution forbids this. They can at best serve as a goal toward which media owners strive and a standard by which one can evaluate local news organizations.

John L. Hulteng explains how important it is that news media assume responsibility in the context of modern industrialization, urbanization, and social and educational changes:

> Under the libertarian theory, it was possible to tolerate biased, distorted, or one-sided presentations because there were many channels; the distortions would balance out, and reality would be discernible. But the social responsibility theory recognizes that when there is only one game left in town, it must be an honest one. Unless those few channels that are available to us provide an accurate, complete flow of news and information, how else can we hope to get a true picture of the world around us, and acquire a basis for making the decision expected of us in a democratic society?[9]

As the libertarian theory developed amidst social changes and its assumptions came under scrutiny, styles of reporting also began to change. In the early twentieth century the pad-and-pencil reporter, like a recorder of objective facts, rushed to the telephone in a race to be the first with a story. But amidst social and educational changes, as well as those in press theorizing, journalists began to go beyond mere reporting of facts to probe the story in depth. Walter Lippmann, who was the editor of the *New York World* in the early twentieth century, once explained:

> When I first went to work on a newspaper, which was after World War I, the generally accepted theory was that it was the duty of the news columns to report the "facts" uncolored by "opinion" and it was the privilege of the editorial page to express opinions about what was reported in the news columns. To this simple rule of the division of labor between reporters and editorial writers, we all subscribed. In practice we all, reporters and editorial writers, broke the rule and this led to many disputes, good-natured and some not so good-natured. The news columns would have opinions with statements of fact that the news editor had not certified. In the course of time most of us have come to see that the old distinction between fact and opinion does not fit the reality of things . . . the modern world being so very complicated and hard to understand, it has become necessary not only to report the news but to explain and interpret it.[10]

This lack of distinction has led to what is called "interpretive" reporting in which the journalist does an investigation into an event or series of events and in his report explains, gives background information, analyzes, and interprets or explains the meaning of the event. An example of such reporting was the Woodward and Bernstein investigation of the Watergate break-in.

Though the theory of social responsibility dominates the mass media in America today, there are still many in the field of journalism who hold to the libertarian theory, believing the press owes nothing to the public and that objective journalism is quite possible. Actually, as we have seen, the social responsibility theory is nothing more than a development and modification of the earlier libertarian theory, and since this is so, we can expect that the issues, the various positions, and the debates will occur within the same general framework.

For a complete picture of the current state of the press, it is important to recognize a fourth theory which characterizes the Soviet press today. While the libertarian theory was a reaction against the former authoritarian one, the Soviet communist theory developed out of the authoritarian concept of the press. Rooted in Marxist determinism and committed to maintaining and expanding the Marxist ideology, the Soviet press is state-owned and state-controlled; it is the voice of the ruling party.[11]

Even a rudimentary history of theories of the press shows how the press has always been and remains today a demonstration of the social and political structures of a given time. The press is grounded in the belief system, the faith commitment, of the society in which it operates. Questions concerning human nature, the relation of humans to society and state, and the basis of knowledge and truth are essential to any understanding of the press. Today's mass media is no exception.

American News Media

In our democratic/capitalist society, the news organizations carry a dual personality. On the one hand, they are part of a "quasi-public" institution protected by the First Amendment; on the other, they are private enterprise operating in a competitive economy. They, therefore, must see themselves as information providers who produce a money-making product, and their audiences as consumers. They must think in terms of meeting consumer needs for information. Traditionally, the basic roles of the news media have been to 1) inform, 2) influence, 3) entertain, and 4) foster development of the nation's economy through advertising, which also provides revenue for the news business. More recently, as a response to meeting consumer needs, a fifth has been added: to serve people and help make their lives better.

The mass media in this country consists of newspapers, newsmagazines, radio and television. Each medium has certain advantages and disadvantages. For instance, television surpasses the other media with its ability to present the news as it happens with dramatic effects of sight, sound and action. Viewers can see the facial expressions of a candidate during a political speech, sit on the 50 yard line of the Super Bowl, or witness the horrors of war at home in their living rooms. Radio, too, can present news as it happens, but it lacks the visual impact of television. The strength of radio is that it requires little listener effort; it can become a companion while the listener does other things. Also, the flexible format of radio allows the station to put news on the air with less apparent interruption than in television programming. However, although both of these media report the who, what, when, and where of major news stories first, they cannot, due to time limitations, concentrate on the why and how of these stories (except for special programming). Unable to touch on the complicated questions of what stories mean to individuals in the audience, the content of a prime time television program actually cannot fill one page of a full-sized newspaper.

Newsmagazines, though not able to cover the news as it happens, have more time between deadlines to gather information and more space in which to present detailed analyses of events. The indepth coverage of issues allows the newsmagazines to compete because they can provide information people cannot get from other sources. This is the case not only for national coverage, but for the thousands of magazines that specialize in, for example, children, teenagers, parents, sports, hobbies, fitness, business, politics, religion, and so forth. Magazines can also provide entertainment through condensed books, short stories, and other features.

Newspapers, though lacking the depth of magazines, do provide more details than do electronic media and also a wider variety of news and information than the other media. Newspapers especially provide extensive coverage of national, regional and local news, classified advertisements, and are particularly effective at covering issues and motivating action at the local level.

Despite differences in the news media, which certainly influence the style each has of presenting the news, they address common questions on the nature of newstelling. First, it must be decided, what is "news"? Is it news when the postman is bitten by your neighbor's dog? Should the Monday morning headlines read, "Local Boys Find New Life," when three teenagers convicted of shop-lifting surrender their lives to Jesus Christ at a Sunday evening evangelistic service? Why is the dating history of a movie actress' daughter kept up to date on the covers of newsmagazines, while most young

women only get a small picture in the pages of the local
newspaper on their wedding day? What constitutes news?

What Makes Headlines?

Generally speaking, news is any information which
someone has not previously received. Most news stories tend
to be concerned with situations and events of the immediate
past, the present, or the future, which interest large numbers
of people. From a more journalistic approach, Herbert J.
Gans offers this definition of news:

> I view news as information which is transmitted from
> sources to audiences with journalists—who are both
> employees of bureaucratic commercial organizations
> and members of a profession—summarizing, refin-
> ing, and altering what becomes available to them
> from sources in order to make the information
> suitable for their audiences.[12]

An important ingredient in this understanding of news information is that the news story is selected by the editor and
shaped by the professional journalist who then presents the
information to the audience. This shaping of the news will
vary with the news organizations involved and will be determined by the editor whose understanding provides the definition of what news is. Philip Schlesinger has said that the news
is, among other things, "the exercise of power over the interpretation of reality."[13] In other words, the newsworthiness of
the various stories of the day and how those selected stories
will be presented to the audience is determined largely by the
professional journalists.

Because of the dual personality of the news institution
and its historical/philosophical roots, the tendency has been
to find and determine which stories are most important and
interesting to the largest number of people. Because of the
audience/profit competition the private-enterprise news
organizations encounter, and their place in a democratic setting, where supposedly there is a variety of faith-
commitments among the people, stories are chosen and
presented from a "lowest common denominator" perspective
which will encompass the values and belief of the largest
number of people. It is assumed, for instance, when a
newscaster says certain values have been violated, that the
audience shares these same values. News about a corrupt
politician implies that the audience believes politicians

should be honest. But it is not quite that simple. In this lowest common denominator fashion, certain values have come to dominate the gathering and presenting of the news in America. Essentially, these are altruistic democracy, responsible capitalism, individualism, and modernism.[14] Combined, these values construct an unstated American ideal which largely determines what will be the news and how it will be presented to the American audience. The news measures reality against this democratic ideal, and people and activities are considered newsworthy in so far as they are an affirmation and/or realization of the ideal, or a deviation from the ideal. Actually, the ideal is a particular view of life that colors and shapes the journalistic interpretation of reality and presentation of events. Here are ways these values are demonstrated in the news.

The first, altruistic democracy, is seen explicitly in foreign news, in that American democracy is shown to be superior to authoritarian governments. American news, like the news in other countries, values its own nation above all others. Therefore, in foreign news coverage, other countries are measured according to American standards and practices. The news can be critical of domestic conditions, but more often these conditions are treated as deviations from the American ideal, with the implication that the ideal still remains workable despite the deviation. This is actually a defense of democratic theory against the inevitable shortcomings of democratic practice. Domestic news, almost like a schoolteacher, explains how American democracy should work by focusing on stories that deviate from the ideal—corruption, conflict, protest, and bureaucratic failings—and applaud those who are honest, efficient, and demonstrate an unselfish interest in the welfare of others. Herbert Gans uses racial integration as an illustration of a norm for democratic living to which the news devotes attention.

> Because citizens are expected to live up to these norms altruistically and because the norms are viewed as expressions of public interest, the violations of the legal and political rights of blacks in the South were news even before supporters of the civil-rights movement began to demonstrate. While attention has now shifted largely to the North, the election of any black official continues to be news, since it is treated as an affirmation and realization of the official norm.[15]

Conversely, those who reject the democratic norm, in this case integration, are labeled as activists, extremists, or militants by the national media, while those equally involved in active support of integration are described as moderates. In some local areas, these labels might actually be reversed.

In his discussion of the enduring values in the news, Gans defines "responsible capitalism" as "an optimistic faith that in the good society, businessmen and women will compete with each other in order to create increased prosperity for all, but that they will refrain from unreasonable profits and gross exploitation of workers or customers."[16] Here, in a romanticized fashion, the family owned business represents the ideal. Unions and consumer organizations are counterbalances for business. Stories on the "welfare state," which offers assistance to those people who cannot work or those who suffer under the pressures of inflation, tend to emphasize problems and failures rather than successes. Foreign news criticizes and concentrates on the economic, political and cultural problems of communist and socialist countries.

One of the most important values in the American view of life is the rugged individualist, the "Rocky" Balboa type. The news focuses on individual people, rather than groups, searching for heroes and heroines during disasters, conquerors (but not destroyers) of nature, and self-made men and women who overcome the obstacles of life, such as poverty or "city hall." Still, despite the respect for the individual, the news discourages anything that happens in excess or is taken to an extreme. This virtue of moderation applies to the gambit of human affairs, ranging from religion (atheists are extremists and too much religion makes one a fanatic) to the college campus (students should study, but those who play too much or are bookworms both receive disapproval). Both excess and abstinence are considered wrong, with moderation in all things the valued norm.

A Faith Behind the Story

What all this amounts to is the construction of a world view, dominant among journalists in the American news process, and identical to the mainstream assumptions of American society. It is an optimistic faith hidden behind every news story, that men and women are ultimately good and will, altruistically, make the right decisions for the betterment of society. Through the competition of these good-natured people in the free enterprise system, prosperity will increase and trickle down to the poor. It is the individual who is most important, who cannot be overrun by nation or society, lest our democratic freedoms be lost. But all things in moderation! It is fine to believe in God, but let's not mix politics or business with religion. Each area has its own section in the newsmagazines.

It is this one dominant view of the world and life activities that saturates every page of the newspaper, influencing everything from the thrust of the headlines to the "religion" section tucked further back in the pages. The entire paper is a daily publication of what is going on in the world, as understood by journalists who hold a certain perspective on life, like a measuring stick, next to each event. Some events are determined to be important and positive if they are an affirmation or realization of this ideal; other events are seen to be unimportant and negative if they are harmful to or deviate from this ideal. The events are then reported as such, with the assumption that the majority of the people in the audience also believe in this same standard for evaluating events and situations, or share the same basic common values and convictions.

Considering the history, basic assumptions, and ideals of the American press, it is understandable that when one view of life comes to dominate the news process, those involved might hail their work as neutral or objective since they represent the mainstream assumptions of the society. Gans explains:

> Like social scientists and others, journalists can also feel objective when they assume, rightly or wrongly, that their values are universal or dominant. When values arouse no dissent or when dissent can be explained away as moral disorder, those who hold values can easily forget that they are values.[17]

Several contemporary newsmen have spoken on the subjects of objectivity in journalism and the dominant world view in the American news process.[18] On questions of selectivity and objectivity in journalism, David Brinkley, of NBC (now ABC), said: "News is what I say it is. It's something worth knowing by my standards."

John Secondari, of ABC, said: "It's absolutely impossible to write a broadcast or put together pictures without having a point of view."

Gerald Green, of NBC, said: "It's impossible not to have a point of view. Once you start selecting facts and choosing what and whom to put on the air, a point of view is implicit."

Bill Moyers, of ABC (now CBS), said: "Of all the myths of journalism, objectivity is the greatest."

In regard to a single world view dominating the news process, Fred Freed, of NBC said:

> This generation of newsmen is a product of the New Deal. Those beliefs of the New Deal are the beliefs that news has grown on. This is true of the networks, of *Newsweek*, of *The New York Times*, of all media.
>
> Men of like mind are in the news. It is provincial.
>
> The blue and white collar people who are in revolt now do have cause for complaint against us. We've ignored their point of views. It's bad. It's bad to pretend that they don't exist.
>
> We did this because we tend to be upper-middle-class liberals. We think the poor are "better" than the middle class. We romanticize them. The best thing that happened to me was a month I spent working in the Detroit slums after the riots. I stopped romanticizing the poor.
>
> I've come to understand that it's really the same with all classes. You've got to sit down with the cop, with the little storekeeper, and get their views. They're human beings like everyone else. Their attitudes emerge logically from their interests and values. They should be covered that way.

In *The New York Times*, David Jayne said:

> Television news is controlled by a few powerful men who do think alike on most major issues. This control is not manifested . . . in a conspiratorial concerted attempt to present or distort the news according to these men's bias.
>
> But the end product, what's seen and heard on the air, especially in live programming, too often results from these biases. The reason, I suggest, is not conscious prejudice, but the common implicit assumptions influencing the major commentators and producers . . .

There is an establishment point of view shared by the television news elite.

A Christian Response

What are we Christians to make of all this? How are we to respond? Francis Schaeffer explains in *How Should We Then Live?* that the vacuum left by the cultural renouncing of Christian absolutes is being filled by arbitrary absolutes determined by a governing elite. Considering the important role of the press in our democratic history, he offers this warning:

> The newsmakers obviously have tremendous power, and if either the elite captures them or if because of their world view they and the elite coincide, then the media is a ready vehicle for manipulative authoritarianism.[19]

We have seen that the observing, analyzing, and reporting of events is never a neutral activity, but is colored by the world view of the journalism involved. If a decisively non-Christian view of events controls the news information we receive, how are we to be responsibly informed in today's world? Can we rely on the traditional sources such as UPI (United Press International) or AP (Associated Press) to do the research for us and estimate what is important for us to know about our lives today and the history of civilization? Does our eternal framework make a difference in the evaluating and reporting of events? Don McNally illustrates this point:

> It might help to recall the early beginnings of Christianity. Christopher Dawson captures the paradox well: "To the ordinary educated man looking out on the world in A.D. 33 the execution of Sejanus must have appeared much more important than the crucifixion of Jesus, and the attempts of the government to solve the economic crisis by a policy of free credit to producers must have seemed far more promising than the doings of the obscure group of Jewish fanatics in an upper chamber at Jerusalem. Nevertheless there is no doubt today which was the most important and which availed most to alter the lot of humanity." We must discipline ourselves in our own day to view all things through the foolishness of the cross. "The life of the world to come is already stirring in the womb of the present," Dawson writes, but it is certain that the mass media will miss the vital signs. "Apparent success often means spiritual

failure, and the way of failure and suffering is the royal road of Christian progress."[20]

Clearly, it is difficult to determine which events are of most significance, but these will always be determined by the ideology of the news media. For example, most cover stories are economic or political; the idea being that economic and political matters affect the largest amount of people and are most important as regards the direction of history. It is also part of the fourth estate's responsibility. As a result, economic and political decisions are presented as being the ultimate forces in history, and, since problems on local, national, international levels are ecopolitical in nature, it follows that the solutions must also be found in these spheres of human activity. Our hope, then, lies in whether certain legislation is passed.

A question then arises over the distinction between propaganda and information. Of course information is essential to propaganda since the latter must have a reference point in reality. McNally refers to Jacques Ellul in *Propaganda* for a discussion of this:

> Ellul warns that we must not limit our understanding of propoganda to the crude methods employed by the totalitarian regimes. In its more sophisticated manifestations modern propaganda also solicits the participation of the individual. It reinforces his myths and crystalizes his confused thoughts. The concentrated control of a large number of media in a few hands does not necessarily produce propaganda, but it is only through such concentration that a true orchestration of reality can be achieved. Such an orchestration provides a way of looking at the world, a means of making sense of it, a way to order it and assign meaning to it.[21]

McNally continues:

> At the heart of the problem of the propaganda problem is a religious problem: what words are to be authoritative for us? How are we to assign meaning to the events of the day? Where there is no authoritative revelation for life and culture from the living God, the effusions of the media and the pronouncements of the experts rush in to fill the vacuum. Our age has shifted the locale of meaning from God to events . . . A people living by such words

become increasingly impervious to the realities of the Christian faith.[22]

It should be obvious that biased news cannot be replaced by unbiased news. But should Christians consider alternative, multiperspectival news? News that would represent viewpoints and events from various subgroups, minorities, social and education levels, political positions, and faith commitments. What would have to be done in order for this to develop? A beautiful illustration of the possibilities for different perspectives in the news comes from the Third World news situation. As Narinder K. Aggarwala explains, the developing countries depend primarily on the Western news sources for their information. "The style, the content, the treatment, and the perspective of practically all the news flowing in and out of the Third World reflects the personality, preferences, and the needs of the Western media."[23] As a result, the stories selected are those thought to be most interesting to the Western audience and tend to be sensational, dealing with wars, disasters, famine, or riots. The information needs of the Third World are then overlooked. Aggarwala offers this illustration of how news from the perspective of the developing countries better meets their needs:

> For example, Tanzania's effort to organize basic rural health services by using paramedics (the Tanzanian version of "barefoot doctors") may not be "sexy" enough for the Western media, but it does present a model to many developing countries. Similarly, the development of inland fisheries in Nepal, the introduction of animal traction for farming in West Africa, and the establishment of the first forest ranger training institute in Honduras may not warrant Western media attention, but they are of great interest to developing countries, showing, as they do, certain progress in meeting the problems of the Third World.[24]

We need to realize, as Ken Heffner points out, "that news does not become Christian by covering only "good" stories or by tacking on a relevant Bible verse to the end of a newscast."[25] The news media must do justice in its reporting to the variety of faith commitments which people hold in our religiously free, democratic society. Jon Kennedy, the author of *The Reformation of Journalism*, says that "criteria for judging daily newspapers (should) include comprehensiveness of coverage, professional ethics, attention to the problems of the oppressed—all minority groups, and an adequate editorial mix, that is, paying attention to the various spheres of the readers' lives in adequately balanced proportion."[26] We must recognize the full implications of the Christian gospel in our life and work together as a community of faith to understand our daily news through the foolishness of the cross.

Notes

1. Herbert J. Gans, *Deciding What's News: A Study of CBS Evening News, NBC Nightly News, Newsweek,* and *Time* (New York: Pantheon Books, 1979), pp. xi-xii.
2. Thomas Schroth, "The Role of the Press in a Democratic Government," in *The Press in Washington,* Ray Eldon Hiebert, ed. (New York: Dodd, Mead & Company), p. 1.
3. Curtis D. MacDougall, *Interpretative Reporting, 4th ed.* (New York: MacMillan Co., 1938, 1963), p. 5.
4. David J. Leroy and Christopher H. Sterling, eds., *Mass News: Practices, Controversies, and Alternatives* (New Jersey: Prentice-Hall, 1973), p. 7.
5. Lester Markel, "Objective Journalism," in *Liberating the Media: The New Journalism,* Charles C. Flippen, ed. (Washington, DC: Acropolis Books, 1974), pp. 77-8.
6. Fred S. Siebert, Theodore Peterson, Wilbur Schramm, *Four Theories of the Press* (University of Illinois, 1956), p. 4.
7. *Report of the Commission of Freedom of the Press, A Free and Responsible Press* (Chicago: University of Chicago Press, 1947).
8. Leroy and Sterling, p. 10.
9. John L. Hulteng, *The Messenger's Motives . . .: Ethical Problems of the News Media* (New Jersey: Prentice-Hall, 1976), p. 12.
10. *The Bulletin of the American Society of Newspapers Editors* (January 1, 1956), p. 7.
11. Siebert, *et. al., Discussion of Soviet-Communist theory of the press.*
12. Gans, p. 80.
13. Philip Schlesinger, "The Sociology of Knowledge" (Paper presented at the 1972 meeting of the British Sociological Assocation, March 24, 1972), p. 4.
14. For a more detailed discussion of these and other values in the news see Gans, p. 42ff.

15. Gans, pp. 44-5.
16. Gans, p. 46.
17. Gans, p. 185-6.
18. The quotations that follow are from Leroy and Sterling, p. 137ff.
19. Francis A. Schaeffer, *How Should We Then Live?: The Rise and Decline of Western Thought and Culture* (New Jersey: Fleming H. Revell, 1976), p. 243.
20. Don McNally, "Our Daily News," *Vanguard*, 10, No. 4 (July-August 1980), p. 6.
21. McNally, p. 5.
22. McNally, p. 5.
23. Narinder K. Aggarwala, "News with Third World Perspectives: A Practical Suggestion"; in *The Third World and Press Freedom*, ed. Philip C. Horton (New York: Praeger Publishers, 1978), p. 197.
24. Aggarwala, p. 199.
25. Ken Heffner, "The Case for an Alternative Christian Radio News Network," *Vanguard*, 10, No. 4 (July-August 1980), p. 13.
26. Jon Kennedy, "The Press: Establishing criteria for evaluating daily metropolitan papers," *New Reformation*, 11, No. 1, (January, 1980), p. 5.

Annotated Bibliography

Flippen, Charles C., ed., *Liberating the Media: The New Journalism*, Washington, D.C.: Acropolis Books, Ltd., 1974.
This book contains arguments by several noted journalists from both the traditional position and the new journalism perspective and shows the influence new journalism has had upon the established media. The contributing authors probe questions such as the "objectivity" of news reporting, the public's rights for access to the media, the injection of the reporters' personal view into news stories, and the effects of the underground press on the media.

Gans, Herbert J., *Deciding What's News: A Study of CBS Evening News, NBC Nightly News, Newsweek, and Time*, New York: Pantheon Books, 1979.
This book examines, among many topics, the values of the news industry, its unspoken ideology, the standards of news judgments, external pressures, and how they

amount to a certain portrayal of America in the news media. This is a thorough work which proposes an alternative in "multiperspectival news."

Horton, Philip C., ed., *The Third World and Press Freedom*, New York: Praeger Publishers, 1978.

This book wrestles with the freedom and responsibility of the press and its relation to Third World countries. Essays investigate and offer alternatives regarding the definition of "good" journalism in the developed world and in the developing world, the challenge to provide more accurate and comprehensive coverage of news from the Third World, and the provision of more accurate and useful information to the developing countries themselves.

Hulteng, John L., *The Messenger's Motives . . .: Ethical Problems of the News Media*, New Jersey: Prentice-Hall, Inc., 1976.

In this book the author explores the news world, examining more than 150 news reports, stories, and broadcasts, focusing on the ethical problems involved in the process of presenting the news. Tracing the development of a news media ethical code, he discusses the current claims of the media and evaluates the successes and failures in the complicated daily lives of news people as regards the stated standards.

Kennedy, Jon, *The Reformation of Journalism: A Christian Approach to Mass Media*, The Craig Press, 1972.

This author sets forth a decisively Christian approach to the mass media by describing the dominant world-life views in existence today and proposing a journalistic mandate as part of the Christian's stewardly task of cultivating God's creation. A number of Christian journals are examined and the response to several questions by the author of selected Christians working in the field are presented. These questions include: "How do you define the role of the Christian press?" "How do you define the role of the Christian as a writer in the public or 'secular' media?" "What is the proper role of the press in evangelizing?"

Siebert, Fred S., Theodore Peterson, and Wilbur Schramm, *Four Theories of the Press*, University of Illinois, 1956.

This collection of essays is a comprehensive study of the mass communication theories that have shaped the media today. Probing the question of why the press is as it is today, this book shows how the historical developments and directions of the "press" are rooted in the basic beliefs and assumptions a society holds regarding the nature of humans, the nature of society and state, the relation of humans to the state, and the nature of knowledge and truth. This is a very important text for the study of the mass media.

Chapter 9

Psychology: A Redeeming Approach

W hen it comes to psychology, contemporary Christians often find themselves at one extreme or the other. Many hold this relatively new field in suspicion because they sense that if our faith is strong we won't have emotional problems. Others have blindly accepted our society's commitment to narcissism and insecurity, assimilating psychology into their view of life without giving it a thorough examination. Both extremes touch on aspects of truth but both naively overlook significant problems with their viewpoints.

The suspicious are right to approach psychology with caution. The history of psychology demonstrates that it has often sought to undermine faith, in general, and Christianity, in particular. Yet, emotions are real and a distinction between emotions and faith must be made clear; neither can substitute for the other. Our feelings and the role they play in how we view ourselves and others are an integral part of what it means to be human. Christians must dedicate themselves to a redeeming approach to psychology, for it has long distorted our view of humanity as created by God.

We cannot go uncritically with the flow of our culture which is inundated with books, talk shows and magazines that promise "five easy steps to self-actualization" or "eight ways to a healthy ego and an awesome sex life." Despite the fact that many such Christian books (written by authors who confess Christ) are designed for use in church groups and as the basis for lay counseling, they are based on the same spirits which dominate popular psychology in our culture. In fact, it is hard to find a difference between the books on the religious and the secular bookshelves. Christians not only have fallen prey to this cultural preoccupation, they have nothing distinctive to say to a world which is looking for help as its idols fail.

Neither of these extremes is satisfactory. As Christians we must build our view of life on a biblical view of humanness. Not only do we need to develop a Christian approach, we also need to master and critique the roots of the dominant trend in psychology—human autonomy.

Clinical Versus Academic Psychology

Whether you want to work in an advertising agency, run for political office, or be a police officer, you are likely to want to use psychology in your occupation. As a consumer, a voter, a parent, or an informed reader of the daily newspaper you should know something of the anthropology (what it means to be human and what makes us so) which is foundational to psychology. So you registered eagerly for the Introduction to Psychology course, or decided to major in psychology. Friends have told you that you are a good listener. You like to help people with their personal problems. You enjoy exploring and figuring out what makes people "tick." But one week into the course, you are beginning to think you never knew what psychology was about. You find out that you will spend the term (and the rest of your life) trailing rats through a maze. You learn to flash a light (stimulus) and count how many times the small rodent will press the bar (response) to get a drop of water. You are promised that in a few terms you'll be able to compute your findings after you take the required statistics course. None of this was what you wanted to learn and it gets clearer by the day that any hopes you had about investigating people's feelings was an illusion. If you raise any questions like "what is psychology anyway?" the grad assistant quickly answers that it is behavioral science: a dedication to watching and measuring quantifiable behavior in its relationship to different stimuli is the only real academic and scientific psychology. What is more, this is the only road to graduate school.

This scenario is not as exaggerated as some might imagine. Apart from a few pockets of "humanistic" or "third force" psychology and a brand-new development that attempts to model computers after human brains in order to understand brains, behaviorism reigns so exclusively in most college and university psychology departments that other types of approaches are not considered psychology. There is tremendous pressure to yield unquestioningly to this one perspective, especially if you desire to pursue academic work beyond the undergraduate level.

The general view of what psychology is and the view of the academic world are so at odds that the shock and disillusionment for a typical freshman can be tremendous. There seem to be only two choices: accept behaviorism or get out of psychology. But behaviorism's monolithic grip should not be confused with the legitimate rigors of scientific work. If a student expects to be trained to do practical therapy without doing any theoretical and experimental work, his or her expectations are illegitimate. Theory and scientific experiments (even with rats) are an integral part of the study of psychology. But even if the freshman shock may seem helpful, the disparity between what the naive public thinks psychology is and what is studied in most academic circles is an indication that something is wrong. There is a rift between clinical psychology (counseling and therapeutic concerns) and academic pyschology. This rift is not merely a matter of individual preferences and hence two branches of psychology. There are at least two different types of activities within this discipline, but this field is divided against itself as to *what psychology is!*[1] That is a serious dilemma. But it is a problem that has its roots in the history of the discipline. How did the two developments split and what drives behaviorism to such dominance in academic circles? The answer to these questions begins with an exploration of the relatively short history of psychology. It is more than mildly ironic that our starting point, an historical overview, is one of the last courses in an undergraduate curriculum.

Even the generally accepted birth-date of psychology betrays the assumptions that have driven this field of inquiry since it has emerged from the womb of philosophy. The advantage of studying something with such a recent history is that every historian of psychology acknowledges its roots in the history of philosophy. But, in spite of these origins, most fix its beginnings with Wilhelm Wundt (1832-1920) because he was able to develop a scientific, *experimental*, approach for psychology. This issue has not just been an overwhelming and seldom questioned influence. It has in fact *defined what psychology is*.

It would be a mistake to suggest that something is inherently wrong with experimentation *per se*. That is not the point here. However, following the development of science in general, and psychology in particular, out of 17th century western philosophy, we see the helpful tool of observational experimentation being formed into an idol. We cannot be comprehensive here. Instead, we trace certain motifs (like the type of experimentation mentioned above) that caused the study of psychology to choose certain paths of development over others. You may recognize elements here that are common to other chapters of this book; that is an indication of how spirits of an age function across many different dimensions of our lives.

A Little Bit of History

Psychology is derived from two Latin words, "psyche" meaning "soul" and "logos" meaning "law for." Psychology identifies a concern to study the law for the soul (what it is and how it operates). The general, unquestioned assumption has been that humans are composed of two basic parts: a body (our physical, material self) and a soul (everything we are that is not concrete and is divine). Aristotle, the ancient Greek philosopher, believed that the soul drove the body. He believed it was composed of three elements: 1) *nutritive*, or consumption and reproduction; 2) *sensitive*, or perception, desire and locomotion; and 3)*rational*, or thought. This view of humanness was largely embraced by Christian theology in spite of being contradictory to a biblical understanding of humanness which portrays humanity as a whole, unseparated, and *integrated* unity.[2] The whole person has different facets, dimensions (ways of being), but not "parts" to be further dissected (a good source for what might be called anthropology done "Christianly" is: *Views of Man and Psychology—Some Readings* by Arnold DeGraaff).

René Descartes (1596-1650), a French philosopher, also divided soul from body, but proposed that not all of our material experience actually originates in our abstract soul. Descartes' formulations began two key threads that we will see woven through philosophy and psychology from this point on. First we see a decreasing role of the soul concept and increasing role of the body concept. He declared that the body had a measure of independence; both sensitive and nutritive aspects are bodily functions that humans shared with animals. The remaining rational work of the soul makes humans different.[3]

Second, Descartes speculated that our bodily functions are driven hydraulically through the nerves. This was consistent with and furthered a 17th century phenomena, "mechanism," which saw reality as a complex machine. He anticipated reflex theory, with its involuntary, automatic muscle responses. The body became a machine that moved itself. This view reflected the love affair of this period in history with the machine, the innovation that was revolutionizing the culture of the time. This view also complimented the belief of the rest of the intellectual community that "matter in motion constituted the only objective reality in the world."[4]

Very rapid changes in philosophy followed, not the least of which was the greater emergence of questions of epistemology, "How do we know?" The British empiricists were committed to the view that the mind grows through experiences of the senses. Both John Locke (1632-1704) and George Berkeley (1685-1753) contributed at this point of discussion. They contradicted Descartes' view, that some ideas are innate, i.e., present at birth. Locke stated that our minds, blank at birth are imprinted with sensations and reflections which merge to form simple ideas which in turn form complex ideas (note again the mechanistic, building-block mentality which dominates the age). In this way, complex ideas are open to analysis, laying the foundation for early experimental psychology and modern behaviorism.

According to this line of thought, ideas were like particles of material. They could agree and form complex ideas or disagree and repel. These are clear reflections of Newton's laws of physics, with physical properties transferred into the realm of ideas. "Indeed, it is possible to see the whole of Locke's psychology as a kind of Newtonian cosmos in miniature."[5]

Locke held that qualities were either primary, that is, they exist whether we perceive them or not (like size and shape), or secondary, they exist in our perception of them. Berkeley carried Locke's thought one step further, asserting that there were no primary qualities. He asserted that ideas had only secondary qualities, and so our certainty is in our perception of things. It is important to understand that he was not saying that an object's existence depends on our perception of it. The issue here is of certainty and this is how Berkeley is a key example of a trend of thought: "All we know is what we see." These philosophers, in striving to understand how we know, adopted the popular view that reality is to be studied empirically (by our experience), atomistically (by finding basic, simple ideas) and mechanistically (by working assumption that our minds like the rest of reality operate like a machine).

The physicians David Hartley (1705-1757) and Julien Offray de la Mettrie (1709-1751) served as key links between 17th century philosophy and the 19th century emergence of experimental psychology. As physicians, both men were well acquainted with and most interested in the body. They both made observations and offered explanations demonstrating that mental activity, instead of being separate, is actually a part or aspect of physical activity. De la Mettrie wrote a rather polemic anti-Christians book, *Man the Machine*. Hartley, though less polemic, gives indication of the far reaching implications of his work for morality and religion in his book *Observations of Man*. Both formulated theories of the physical roots of mental processes. We find in Hartley and de la Mettrie louder echoes of Newtonian physics which are readily acknowledged (rather than implied). So we see that Descartes' move to allow some independence of the body from the soul became a total assimilation of the mind (the new term for soul) by the physical (body). Hartley went so far as to explain the physical cause of thought as a transfer of vibrations through the nervous system to create brain vibrations, the physical counterparts of ideas. It was as if something in the atmosphere of this period of history drove these men and others to deny a radical division and the preeminence of the soul/mind over the body. But the force of it drove them beyond a good critique of Aristotle's view of humanness to a not-so-gradual materialization of humanity: "What you see is what you get!"

Gustav Fechner (1801-1887) believed that all of reality was a continuous system: Mental objects (consciousness) and material objects (organized matter) differed only in degree of organization. He sought to identify the two quantitatively. In our history, he figures as the formulator of the basis for experimental psychology. His own academic background was originally in physics. He used the law of "just noticeable differences" for sensation measurement, developed by a physiologist (Weber), and established a functional relationship beween stimulus and sensation. Richard Lowry, an historian of psychology, writes of Fechner's contribution:

> But the important thing, he (Fechner) considered, was not whether "Weber's Law" held true in every case, but rather that it was a first step in the right direction . . . to make psychology an exact, experimental science after the fashion of physics. Whether this *direction* was a feasible one in which to proceed is not at issue; suffice it to say that Fechner's conviction took root, in a soil that was prepared for it, . . . it has endured undiminished, even up to this day.[6]

The direction Lowry mentions is *precisely* the issue for us. This author had driven the last nail for our construction of the case for the foundational preoccupations of psychology. Fechner, along with many other noted individuals, was deeply affected by the work of Hermon von Helmholtz who suggested a principal of constancy for physiological forces. Sigmund Freud (whose work will be cited later in the chapter) was another intellectual strongly influenced by Helmholtz's work. Lowry's comment about "root" and "soil" serves as a capstone to this portion of our study.

In post-Renaissance Europe, scientific dominance resulted in more than an emphasis on sensory data. It was formally accepted that certainty could be grounded only in what was sensed, what was observable. When Greek metaphysics was rejected, the dominance of the soul was denied. This led to the autonomy of the body and then to a materialization of the mental. This trend was directed by a cultural infatuation with the machine and mechanical things in general. That infatuation became a complete reordering of things according to Newtonian physics: complex ideas and phenomena are built from simpler ones. The result was that analysis became breaking a thing down to its smallest building blocks. Physics and chemistry experiments were being designed and performed according to very precise measurements, and this mathematical precision ruled the day as the only acceptable scientific data.

As a result of these developments, psychology became a specific scientific model for *method* and *procedure*, and so changed the dominant view of human nature. The *content* area of psychology became: 1) Humans and animals function as well-oiled machines with only slight differences; 2) Humans are products of their environment; and 3) Human nature is basically simple, divisible into parts to be understood.

Faith in Psychology as Science

The initiation of Psychology as "new science" (separated at last from philosophy) is credited to a school of thought known now as the structuralists. When Wilhelm Wundt (1832-1920) founded the first experimental laboratory in Leipzig, Germany, there was great excitement surrounding this effort to analyze human consciousness. Psychology's objective was to break conscious experience down into its component parts with the same experimental precision as the natural sciences. Wundt directed his students to submit themselves to incredible personal rigor in order to analyze accurately their own sensations. This method, called introspection, was a rigid experimental procedure that required as many as 10,000 practice observations in order to be considered skilled enough to participate in gathering valid data. These structuralists in Germany and America (E.B. Tichener studied in Leipzig and began a laboratory at Cornell) are considered the first real psychologists because they were the first experimentalists. This school began to try to imitate Auguste Comte's method (positivism), an objective that persists in the dominant school today, behaviorism. Method is defined by measurability and its precision. The objective of experimentation is to search for the simplest elements and then how they combine and connect with their physiological conditions.

In America, the school of thought that supplanted the structuralists was the functionalist school. This was not a violent break with the European school nor was it a self-conscious beginning. It "evolved" from structuralism's own roots in Darwinism. Functional psychology took exception to the "pure science" approach in Leipzig and Cornell. It shifted the emphasis of its objective toward finding out how the mind functions. It rejected as unprofitable the efforts to pick apart sensory experience, preferring to research the mental processes involved in our adaptation to our environment. The British theory of evolution and the American emphasis on practicality made this psychology what it was. Functionalism did not take exception to any of the *methods* of introspection. Their questions focused on content. Structuralism had been severely limited by its desire to find elements of sensation. Functionalism wanted to understand *how* the mind worked. This shift paved the way for Watson's revolt.

John B. Watson's behaviorism provided for the convergence of functionalism, animal psychology, and objective experimental methods. He made a radical break with the study of consciousness as the content of psychology and with introspection.[7] His "method of psychology" was so sweeping and complete that previous schools, other types of psychology, and many of the social sciences were revolutionized. Watson capitalized on the American emphasis on function and the then-current interest in animal learning and its applicability to humans (both rooted in Darwinism). The age-old pursuit of experimental objectivity still reigned. Watson's key ingredient was the rejection of mind and consciousness.

Behavior is the only aspect of humanness we can accurately (objectively—he meant) observe. We cannot speculate on any workings of the mind and feelings. In order to deal only with tangibles (Berkeley), we now realize we cannot trust even our inner observations (introspections). The public verifiability and repeatability of research came to be paramount for B.F. Skinner, Watson's successor, and other behaviorists. Even though the very core of the meaning of psychology was ripped out of the science, these behaviorists were applauded by their contemporaries.[8] The irony is that the very existence of what once was the focus of the content of the discipline of psychology, "the Law for the soul," is now completely denied in Skinner's behaviorism.

The monolithic grip behaviorism has had and continues to have on American psychology makes superfluous any detailed discussion of it here. The important point is that the method of the science has not only successfully changed the definition of psychology but it has determined the meaning of it. Behaviorism is not just a method by which to understand human nature, it has had the power to discard the one dimension of ourselves that psychology once aimed to study. As a result, psychology has been reduced to the study of observable behavior, and in an effort to be increasingly precise, that behavior is itself broken down into minute physiological responses. Behaviorism as a science is devoted to a view of humanness that is materialistic and mechanistic because that is what we are supposedly able to study with objective precision. However, even behavior is too broad an area of observation. B.F. Skinner's even more radical rendition of behaviorism admits to the final goal—control of human nature. We study behavior because over that we can have tighter experimental control, and now we do it with the societal goal of control of behavior at-large. So the leopard of scientific experimentation finally shows its true and ultimate spots—human autonomy.

There has been great public outcry when Skinner revealed the ultimate conclusions of this faith stance, the grounding of our certainty in what we can observe. We see that it undercuts our dignity. So we turn to other developments in psychology that seem to preserve some humanness. Should a Christian opt instead for the seemingly more palatable Freudian/Jungian school, or Gestalt psychology, or the newest humanist psychologies (often referred to as Third Force Psychologies)? We think not.

Just about the time J.B. Watson was formulating his so-called revolutionary development of behaviorism in the USA, a smaller revolt of a much more radical nature was taking shape in a corner of European psychology. While he was on a vacation, Max Wertheimer (1880-1943) purchased a stroboscope, a child's toy, invented 80 years earlier. This device projected a series of pictures in rapid succession, thus creating a moving picture for any delighted child "scientist." This initial exploration was followed by a set of formal observations at the University of Frankfurt. Wertheimer enlisted the involvement of two other scientists, Kurt Koffka and Wolfgang Kohler. These men worked so closely from this point on that generally they are all three credited with the new school, gestalt psychology. Slits of light were successively projected at different angles. At slower rates Kohler and Koffka saw two separate lines. At a fast rate they observed a single stationary line. But at a rate of approximately 60 milliseconds the two projections were seen as a single line moving.

This last occurrence called the "phi phenomenon" could not be explained or accounted for by the Wundtian framework. The structuralists trained themselves to observe their own perceptions in constituent parts or elements. This technique and objective of experimentation rested on the assumption that sensations are really combinations of separate simpler elements. Wertheimer and company found a sensation that couldn't be analyzed into elements. The moving line was a whole that was different from the sum of its parts. The other basic assumption of the structuralists was that there is a one-to-one correspondence of external events and human perception of them (associationism—with roots in British empiricism). Again, the moving line, observed the gestaltists, doesn't fit the reigning perspective. So, the seeds of refutation for the structuralists are sown.

Gestalt psychologists assert that complex mental experience cannot be broken down into simpler parts, for the whole has a character of its own that is lost when divided into its components. This wholistic approach seems attractive when we see the terrible results of the fragmentation of behaviorism. But we need only to look a little closer and we find out that even this wholeness is formulated from an understanding of physics, force fields, that was coming to prominence in the late 19th century. The phenomenological method which gestalt psychologists use could be a useful alternative to the scientific method. It emphasizes a use of naive (undivided and untrained) experience to take in the totality of a phenomenon. But deeper examination reveals a basic assumption of certainty founded in experience; and our certainty as Christians cannot be grounded in naive experience.

Interestingly enough, these early gestaltists did not spawn a clearly defined new theoretical school. Subsequent psychologists owning this heritage generally reflect only the basic root in a contra-analytical frame of reference that fosters a wholistic assumption and results in a phenomenological methodology. What this "alphabet soup" term means (for our discussion here) is that experimental psychology should approach phenomena (things we experience) as wholes. Breaking these wholes into elements actually destroys or at least distorts the meaning of the events. Beyond this basic approach there is no real coherence to gestalt psychology as there is to structuralism and behaviorism. We also find it fascinating that the gestalt challenge to the assumptions of analytical science did not really shake the foundations of mainstream psychology. As clearly radical (to the root) as their break was, gestaltists to this day are perceived as odd and peripheral by most basic psychology texts, if they are mentioned at all. This is further evidence of the mainstream commitment, commitment no less than faith in analytical science. The early gestaltists opened "Pandora's box." As these released spirits fly around shooting darts, their efforts remain scattered and ineffective against the reigning views in experimental psychology.

What might be a biblically founded Christian response to gestalt psychology? Clearly we can affirm this blow struck near the heart of the mainstream idol. The gestaltists exposed the limits of analysis. They offered an approach that allowed for wholeness and stood against the trend for control and the fragmentation of behaviorism. But we must also recognize where this framework does not offer a well-rounded critique. We should not be surprised to find that gestalt psychology is historically rooted in a more general movement of thought that was finding fault with Newtonian physics. Kohler moved away from the idea that viewed physical reality as reducible to parts and toward recognition of forces. But he argued strongly that pyschology must ally itself with physics. So the gestaltists don't really help psychology break from the physical sciences. They merely reflect new trends in the physical sciences. Further, as they refute analysis and superficial abstraction favoring a wholistic and contextual viewpoint, gestaltists still seek a free and unbiased description of immediate experience as it occurs. This reflects a continued trust in (albeit naive) experience that Christians can't accept.

One of the first issues most freshman psychology students learn to get straight is the difference between psychoanalysis and experimental psychology. The current disdain for counseling psychology of any sort is best symbolized by the common reference to experimental psychology as *academic* psychology. The clear implication is that all else is nonacademic (and of course inferior). This chauvinistic attitude is just one more reflection of the impact of empiricism on this discipline. The psychoanalytic school as it began with Sigmund Freud (1856-1939) was augmented by an influx of trained counseling psychologists that rose in response to a post-World War II need for psychological help for veterans. Together they form the clinical side of psychology. Most counselors receive basic education in experimental psychology, and then appropriate one of the myriad of counseling techniques, usually via graduate school. Even in counseling clinics, emphasis on research is growing. The clinicians (who are not psychoanalysts) tend to hold to a perspective fostered and nurtured by the experimental mainstream (usually behavioristic). The counseling technique they adopt structures their view of reality. Compassionate therapists nearly always reflect a grounding belief in the goodness and autonomy of humanity, and they most often seek a wholistic approach.

We'll focus here on psychoanalysis because it offers such a distinctive view of human nature. Because the psychoanalysts seem to favor the study of certain innate aspects of our nature instead of emphasizing our environment, we are drawn to them. At least they work with the mental processes denied by the behaviorist. Because they are concerned with feelings, we are drawn to hope that this perspective could actually prepare us to help people. But if we take even a cursory look at the roots of this tradition, we find an equal devotion to a natural science model. Freud was as influenced by physics as were the mainstream experimentalists. There is clear evidence that he used Newtonian laws of attraction and repulsion to explain the operation of our unconscious. "We need not look far though, to find that those physicalistic principles to which Freud gave expression in the project (a finally abandoned effort to formulate a systematic theory of nerve force) were to recur time and again in later psychological writings" (parenthesis is ours).[9] It is more than a mild irony that the school of thought often juxtaposed to behaviorism is just as rooted in mechanistic science.

However, in contrast to behaviorism's materialism, the psychoanalytic school continued to deal with a framework of consciousness and the unconscious. Freud has had basic influence even in experimental circles on developments of areas such as motivation and child psychology. His work has promoted a general recognition that rationality has been overemphasized in our explanations of human behavior. Neo-Freudians like Adler have formed individualistic theories of emotional development. However, on the whole psychoanalytic methodology has been held in disdain by experimental psychology; it is said to be too subjective. There are also new trends, which Christians applaud, that challenge the drive for total objectivity that is the basis for this disdain.

A third potential option is humanistic psychology. It tantalizes us with rather scathing critiques of the dominant orientation to facts alone. Some critiques even question the existence of mere neutral unconnected facts. Humanistic psychology emphasizes experience, and relies on the modern philosophical trends of existentialism for its roots. Radical subjectivism is clearly opposed to radical objectivism, but it is not a biblical view of reality. We can rely on humanistic psychologists to ask penetrating questions of mainstream psychology that no one in it is able to ask. We can and should follow their somewhat courageous willingness to "go against the flow." It is even possible that their demands for plurality within the discipline will create some room for the legitimacy of a biblical approach. But we can't accept their frameworks either.

Christian Psychology

So what can we do to confess Christ in psychology? We can offer critique. But we must be careful that it's not a cheap critique full of shallow analyses and half truths. An example might be this: "Behaviorism is based on the experimental use of rats because behaviorists believe humans are just the highest animal form. Christians don't believe humans are just the highest animal form. Christians don't believe in evolution so I can't be a 'rat runner.' It undercuts the God given dignity of humanity!" There is nothing untrue *per se* in this agrument. But it fails to address the real problem of experimentation, concern for objectivity. A better way to address the concern for objectivity is to question even the validity of the notion by examining its root assumptions. Some Christian and secular psychologists are suggesting that subject reflexivity, a subject's effect on an experiment and even the experimenter's reflexivity or bias cannot be removed by any amount of manipulation of independent and dependent variables. So rather than falsely denying their existence, let's take them into account—own up to them so to speak—making for a much truer observation in the long run.[10]

In light of the drastic wrong turn psychology took toward behaviorism, we could bring great *shalom* to the discipline by figuring out what it is that psychology should study. Arnold DeGraaff[11] has suggested that we should focus on emotions and their constituents, sensations and feelings. This is a unique dimension of human nature that can not be reduced to biology or chemistry. Nor can it be confused with social interactions like politics or economics. There is an emotional side to these activities but they are more and different in a fundamental way than feelings. If we allow psychology to be reduced to physiology or chemistry we buy into a model of humanness that denies the rich diversity of who we are. So, to suggest to secular psychology that we should be studying the realm that is rightfully ours could be quite literally to save it from its own self-destruction. Isn't this after all how this chapter began? Instead of an introductory psych student ten or twenty years from now being disillusioned about learning to help people, he or she could learn of a whole school of psychology that says it is the study of our emotional life (complete with experiments), a study that doesn't give up on emotionality because it can't be studied the same way that we study physics.

In order to be psychology students in ways that are consistent with our Christian commitment, we must be willing to question the truth of both how the discipline defines itself and how it manifests that definition by its methodology (for research). The beginning of such questioning is with an understanding of how psychology is shaped in both content and method by dominant cultural forces. Next we must discern in which ways those forces are and are not in the service of Christ. For example, as we have traced the development of psychology as a distinct science, one of the recurring themes has been the study of "parts" of perception or behavior that can be isolated by making quantifiable observations. Both the study or parts to understand the whole and the pressure to express it by precise measurement reflect a view of reality that has been sweeping through western culture since the Enlightenment.

Among several assumptions mentioned throughout this chapter, this view of reality holds two which are essential: the most certain knowledge we can have of any particular object is gained by measuring it; and the whole is equal to the sum of its parts. There were the key discoveries that empowered the development of the physical sciences. However, as Christians, we know that whole people are not simply equal to the sum of their parts. People have dimensions or ways of being that can be concentrated upon and studied, but to do that with integrity we must be continually conscious of how these aspects can be understood only as they relate to others. Measurement is a useful tool because it allows us to be definitive. But we also know that there is no certainty in such definition.

We have seen how, time and again the development of psychology as a science has depended upon trust in these two assumptions. Certain things, to the exclusion of others, were studied because they could be measured objectively and precisely. Those things were divided into parts in order to be manageable. The underlying drive for human control has tones of arrogance and autonomy. Psychology became the study of behavior because behavior could be divided and measured precisely. Other real things about humanity were either ignored or, as in Skinner's work, their existence was denied.

These are the types of assumptions and trust in them that must be challenged. We can form theories and investigate them in ways that are not motivated by a drive for precision and objectivity. Such investigations may leave us without the sense of control that those tools give us, but it is time to be liberated from their dominance. Our psychic lives are so much richer than observable behavior. How much more fun and fulfilling would it be to study psychology as it is rather than as we must remake it to fit a scientific framework developed for the sake of false notions of certainty. Christians could bring fresh air to this field if they would only have the courage to throw open the doors and windows. But there is tremendous risk involved. The reigning view of science engenders such tunnel vision that we may be considered fools for entertaining the notion that doors and windows and especially fresh air even exist. But such radical departures from the status quo are required by what we believe.

A biblical view of human nature must be the foundation of the departure. We can begin with the assumption that God created whole people who cannot be perceived as merely the sum of their parts.

As long as we continue to think that our psychic dimension can be reduced to biological, chemical, physical elements we can never understand what is uniquely psychic. Arnold DeGraaff[12] has suggested that there is a dimension of humanness that is basically sensation, feeling and emotion that cannot be broken down into more fundamental physical properties. There is no greater certainty to be gained about sensations themselves by studying chemical changes in the brain. There is, of course, a way in which our feelings are related to chemical balance or imbalance, but those feelings are wholly defined as feelings. A psychologist's job is to focus on the feelings as feelings and not as a conglomerate of chemical reactions. Can we be satisfied to believe that feelings are feelings and that no great certainty is to be gained by "discovery" of their more "basic" chemical make-up? As we have seen, such "discoveries" are actually distortions (or even a denial) of the feelings themselves. So the plea is to let psychology be psychology. Christians can choose to base their research on this assumption or we can continue to follow secular assumptions. One path leads to exciting new vistas. The other will help perpetuate a false view of reality that is quickly being recognized as the dead end that it is, even in secular circles.

A second fundamental departure can be in the methodology we choose for experimental research in psychology. Mary Stewart Van Leeuwen and Mary Vander Goot[13] have each taken slightly different approaches to challenge the basic drive for objectivity in psychological research methodology. They suggest a new paradigm that is based on a fundamental acceptance of the researcher and subject's own impact on the experiment's results. The historical development of psychology has assumed that total objectivity could be achieved, and so the research method has striven to factor out things like the experimenter's expectations and the subject's suspicions. Concealing the true purpose of the study from the subjects and "double blind" designs (neither the subjects nor the experimenters know which subjects are the control group) are classic examples of attempts to eliminate the influence of the subject and the experimenter on the process and results of the study. The question must be asked: *Can* these influences be eliminated? Or are we chasing after models of research design that can't be applied to the study of psychology in order to perpetuate the myth that psychology must be like physics in order to be truly scientific?

This issue of subject reflexivity (his or her ability to reflect on the event) is being raised even by some non-Christian psychologists. There is liberation in accepting the reality of reflexivity in psychological research and developing experimental designs that utilize it. But this requires that we give up the false attempts of absolute control through false notions of objectivity. Again, such radical changes in our orientation to what scientific research is, will require an uncommon bravery. But can we do anything different, given our foundational beliefs about the nature of humanness? To be human is to reflect, and no amount of manipulation of experimental procedure can make such reflection disappear.

As a final word we can suggest that departures such as the ones briefly proposed above can bring healing to the study of psychology. Even the mainstream of this discipline is beginning to acknowledge that there is a crisis in psychology today.[14] There is a decreasing consensus on what psychology is. We can see that this disintegration is a result of its historic effort to try to emulate the physical sciences. DeGraaff's proposal aims at letting psychology be psychology, not reduced to physics or blown out of proportion to include all of behavior. Vander Goot and Van Leeuwen's proposal provides a concrete suggestion for acknowledging something that is fundamental to the psychic dimension of our lives—reflection. Even the historic divorce of counseling and experimentation can be somewhat bridged by abandoning false notions of objectivity. There is a legitimate difference between the practice of counseling and the practice of experimentation. But counseling techniques have always had to take into account the reflections of the patient. It is even suggested by many that the best methods actually focus on those reflections for the healing process. Traditionally, counseling has revolved around our emotions. Despite the great disdain much of "scientific" psychology has had for psychotherapy, there may be much it can learn from it.

Notes

1. Gary Collins, *The Rebuilding of Psychology* (Wheaton, IL: Tyndale Publishers, 1977), pp. 3-12.

2. William S. Sahakian, *History and Systems of Psychology* (New York: Schenkman, 1975), pp. 9-10.

3. Duane P. Schultz, *A History of Modern Psychology* (New York: Academic Press, 1975, second edition), p. 22.

4. Richard Lowry, *The Evolution of Psychological Theory: 1650 to the Present* (New York: Aldine-Atherton, 1971), p. 9.

5. Lowry, p. 21.

6. Lowry, p. 101.

7. Schultz, p. 177.

8. Schultz, p. 207.

9. Lowry, p. 144.

10. Experimental reflexivity is the topic of two papers from the Calvin Center for Christian Studies (Calvin College) presented at the Institute for Christian Studies (Toronto), June 1982: Mary Stewart Van Leeuwen, "Reflexivity in North American Psychology: Historical Reflections on One Aspect of a Changing Paradigm," and Mary Vander Goot, "Inquiry and Context." Similar topics were addressed by both women at JUBILEE 1983 (Pittsburgh, PA), Vander Goot, "Psychology and Responsibility," and Van Leeuwen, "The Mouse that Roars: A Fresh Look at Human Nature in a Changing Psychology." Both tapes are available from Thompson Media, Stahlstown, PA 15687.

11. Arnold DeGraaff, "What is Psychology" (monograph available from the Institute for Christian Studies, 229 College Street, Toronto, Ontario, Canada M5T 1R4).

12. DeGraaff, pp. 15-17.

13. Again cite further Vander Goot and Van Leeuwen, note No. 10 above.

14. Collins, pp. 6-8.

Annotated Bibliography

Collins, Gary R., *The Rebuilding of Psychology, An Integration of Psychology and Christianity*, Wheaton, IL: Tyndale House Publishers, Inc., 1977.

Collins skillfully shows the internal disintegration of this discipline and makes a plea for a Christian remedy. He covers some issues in the history of psychology and provides a thorough working knowledge of the current breadth of the field. His critique focuses on empiricism, determinism, relativism, reductionism, and naturalism, asserting that, though rarely discussed, presuppositions are extremely important. His chapter end footnotes are very useful, for they refer to secular psychologists who are asking penetrating questions within the field. A student trying to cope with a secular psychology department needs these. It is disappointing that Collins falls back on a view of man that sounds metaphysical at some points and never really offers much as a biblical alternative for psychology. His theistic watchword, "God is the source of all truth," reflects his reference to Donald MacKay. A good critique of how this falls short of a radical Christian approach can be found on JUBILEE 1983 tapes by Vander Goot and Van Leeuwen.

DeGraaff, Arnold, *Views of Man and Psychology in Christian Perspective, Some Readings*, Toronto: Institute for Christian Studies (229 College Street, Toronto, Ontario, M5T 1R4).

DeGraaff has collected a series of articles and essays to begin work on a Christian view of man (anthropology), especially as it relates to psychology. The first five articles provide grounding in issues of anthropology and a particular Christian philosophical tradition's biblically based answers. Fair examinations and critiques of Tournier and Jay Adams (probably the two most widely read Christians in the field) follow. Then DeGraaff brings together his own view for psychology in the form of separate essays and text of lectures. The book ends with an article critiquing the psychoanalytic tradition. A very useful list of readings is included. This is required reading for a serious student of psychology.

Lowry, Richard, *The Evolution of Psychological Theory: 1650 to the Present*, New York: Aldine-Atherton, 1971.

This is a good basic work on the development of

psychology as an academic discipline. Even though the approach is frugal (it's a short book), Lowry captures especially psychology's roots in the mechanistic world view of the Enlightenment of Europe. The book is not an obvious critique, but provides useful background and insight for one. Most university libraries have a shelf for history of psychology. Any student serious about building an understanding of the roots of psychology in secular thought (good points and bad) should read through several of these.

Schultz, Duane P., *A History of Modern Psychology*, New York: Academic Press, 1975.

This is one of the best secular accounts of the history of psychology. Every "school" is addressed, so it serves as a useful reference. Sections of original text (usually "telling" excerpts) accompany clear synopses of that particular theoretical development. What is best about this book is its acknowledgement of "geists" or spirits of an age and how they influence the way psychology chose to develop at several historical points. This is a readable basic text for understanding the history of psychology.

Chapter 10

Power and the Gospel

To be a Christian student is demanding. Double study carries with it a high price tag. It doesn't mean that a Christian student will have no time to enjoy the craziness of college life, or the rewarding involvement in extracurricular activities, or will have to sacrifice time just to relax and enjoy friends. But make no mistake, there is a demand, there is a cost. There will be extra books to read. There will be extra lectures and conferences to attend. There will be endless discussions with fellow students and possibly professors. There will be an emotional strain which comes with the struggle to wade through the material in search of a Christian perspective. Some friends will find it difficult to identify with your passionate quest and others will find your perspective amusing. In short, the weight of being a Christian student has the potential to crush a person. If a person thinks that being a Christian student will in some way qualify him or her as a "super" Christian it is only because he or she has yet to feel the weight of what is being asked.

To consider the demands of being a Christian student should be sobering. The preceding chapters should give you a sense of the breadth of the task that awaits Christian students. The various chapters also give some beginning direction to a number of fields. But is this all the student needs? Is a student who has a sober evaluation of the task and some introductory insights ready to tackle the job of being a Christian in a college? We think a realistic evaluation and good foundation are essential. But if the student approaches this task with no more, he or she is in danger. The Christian student needs to have the entire endeavor energized by the power of God. Lack of that power will lead to the student's eventual failure. To be energized with the power of God, however, is to have the possibility of making significant progress as a Christian student. But what is this power like? How can I have it as a student?

Power and the Gospel

> "Power of the world in His hands,
> Power of the world in His hands,
> Power!"

People applauded and shouted as they finished singing. Indeed, a sense of power did rush through the crowd. A group of three hundred students had come together for an "evangelism" conference. Early in the conference leaders announced, "a lot of conferences talk about evangelism, but at this conference we're going to *do* evangelism." With little more training than a quick review of Christ's life, death and resurrection, the students were sent out on the streets of an urban center. They assembled several hours later to share stories of a variety of encounters, and the reports sounded like a combination of accounts from "Ripley's Believe It or Not" and "The Twilight Zone." But though the experience bordered on the bizarre, a vitality pulsed through the crowd as they gathered to worship. Was this the power of God people were experiencing?

Many believed the freshness, the aliveness they felt had to be the power of God. But was it? If it was, why was it manifest in this circumstance? If this is the power of God, are there other ways to make this power available? These are critical questions. As Christians we confess that all of life is empowered by God. Not just the task of evangelism or the service of worship, but every aspect of life must be empowered by God if it is to be pleasing to Him or experienced in its fullness. Therefore, understanding the nature of God's power could be a key to how effectively we are able to impact the variety of circumstances in which we find ourselves in society. If we are to impact politics, art, technology, or any number of other areas with the healing presence of Christ, we need to be empowered by God.

Power is a subject of great interest in our world today. People vie for, kill for, exploit for, and more deeply, long for power. Though their lives lack for nothing except the power which comes from running the huge oil corporation, J.R. and Bobby Ewing destroy their family in the battle over Ewing Oil (on "Dallas"). Millions watch weekly, vicariously yearning for such power which our routine existences never approach. Part of the alienation of twentieth century America is the inability of most people to have power over the contingences of their work world. The board of directors decides to computerize the corporation. Your job is doomed because a computer is much more efficient than you. The parent corporation determines the product you manufacture can be produced more cost-efficiently in a developing country so your plant is closed and you are out of a job. White collar or blue collar, you don't have the power to control such situations. How do people understand power as it exists in the world around them?

The sense of power which most permeates our world today is the belief that power is the ability to force your will on others or at least to confine others to certain patterns of behavior.[1] Having power is having your way. In surveying many contemporary sociologists, one finds the subject of power prominent. Sociologists assume the nature of power to be the ability to dominate. C. Wright Mills was the sociologist who brought the analysis of power to prominence in contemporary sociology. His most famous work is *The Power Elite*. In a later book he shows that power is to be understood as dominance:

> Power has to do with whatever decisions men make about the arrangements under which they live and about the events which make up the history of their times. The basic problem is who is involved in making the decisions or not making them.[2]

Later Mills further defines power by separating it into three levels: coercion; authority; and manipulation.[3] In each case, power assumes the sense of domination.

Radical historian Gabriel Kolko saw the nature of power lodged in economic structures of a society. He said that all power in America was an aspect of economic power.[4] But underlying his view of power as being a function of the economic structure is still the view that power is the ability to force your will on others. Kolko says that . . . "business is the keystone of power which defines preconditions and functions of the larger American social order."[5] While power resides in the economic structure, the nature of this power is to have its way in the larger society.

Popular culture and academic sociologists affirm the same understanding of power. It would be fair to say that the view that power is the ability to force your will on others or at least confine others to certain patterns of behavior has permeated society. But does this general consensus mean that this is truly what power is? When we speak of power as Christians, is this what we mean? Do Christians acknowledge that the power of God means that He can force His will or confine behavior?

In C.S. Lewis's children's stories, "The Chronicles of Narnia", the great lion, Aslan, is both the symbol of power and the Christ-figure. In *The Magician's Nephew* we are given a curious insight into the nature of Aslan's power. In a dialogue with a character, Digory, we have this description:

> Up till then he [Digory] had been looking at the Lion's great front feet and the huge claws on them [symbolizing Aslan's great power]; now, in his despair, he looked up at its face. What he saw surprised him as much as anything in his whole life. For the tawny face was bent down near his own and (wonder of wonders) great shining tears stood in the Lion's eyes. They were such big, bright tears compared with Digory's own that for a moment he felt as if the Lion must really be sorrier . . .[6]

Aslan's power is curious at this point. While no one would doubt his might or ability to dominate, we see in addition his vulnerability. Tears are not normally associated with power. Has Lewis tried to show us how other qualities can influence power? Is he saying power should be exercised with compassion? If power is the ability to force your will on others or to confine others to certain patterns of behavior, is Lewis giving us an admonition that when we have to exercise power we do it with compassion? No! What Lewis has done takes us much deeper. By focusing on the story's Christ-figure (the lion Aslan), he causes us to see a kind of power that seems ambiguous. It is this confusing sense of power that often confronts us in Scripture. We hear of a "Suffering Servant" or we watch as the Ruler of the Universe is crucified by the people He created. The ambiguity of power in Scripture has often puzzled us. What Lewis reflects, however, is that the Scripture has a different understanding of power. When we approach Scripture with the notion of power as generally understood in our culture, it does puzzle us; but if we allow the Bible to define power itself, we find that the apparent ambiguities begin to clear.

At their root most current definitions of power are negative. It is hard to understand power which forces its will on others as anything but alienating.[7] To force your will is to create dependency within the person or group on which your will is being forced. This dependency is unhealthy and alienating. But we find that from the very beginning of the Bible, power is viewed in a different way. In Genesis 1:28, God confers power upon human beings; we read, "God blessed them and said to them, 'Be fruitful and increase in number; fill the earth and subdue it. Rule (have dominion) over every living creature that moves on the ground!' " And, in Genesis 2:15 we read, "The Lord God took the man and put him in the Garden of Eden to work (cultivate) it and take care of it." Our first observation is that, at least in this context, power is a positive, not a negative thing. Power is graciously given to humans as a way to unlock the potential lodged in the creation. The power people have is to unfold the creation, open it up to what it was intended to be.[8] But to understand power in this positive way means a radical redefinition of our current notions of power.

Human beings are given the positive power to rule or have dominion and to cultivate by God. As theologian Allan Boesak points out, this positive power has two basic elements. First, there is no power in the creation that is not dependent on and reflective of God's power. The first element of power, defined positively, is dependence. We speak here not of power which makes others dependent, but power that is by its very nature dependent on someone else, that is, God. This is borne out by the second element. Boesak says, "Man receives dominion over the rest of creation while he himself is portrayed as utterly defenseless, without protection, without weapons or the means to assert himself."[9] This means that power should not force one's will, but by its very nature power must be *service*. Power given to people is dependent on God and intended to serve the creation. Power that forces its will needs coercion and force to accomplish it. Power which serves finds an open, ready response in a creation which is waiting to have its potential unlocked.

Could it be that society could so thoroughly distort this concept of power so that it has become unrecognizable? The first two chapters of Genesis give us such a different view of power. If Scripture defines power as dependence and service, we will have to transform radically the way we understand power in our world as Christians. But is there further biblical support to suggest that power is not the ability to dominate?

We begin our inquiry with a brief survey of the Old Testament. Several of the major stories seem to confirm our suspicion. The children of Israel were totally at the mercy of the Egyptians. It was the Egyptians who were forcing their rule on the Israelites, whose wish was to leave the country so that they might serve their God. Defenseless and weaponless they seemed to be without power, yet in their dependence they were given power to be free.

Gideon was willing to serve God and immediately found how dependent he was when he was told by God to reduce his army to a few hundred to confront thousands of Midianites. The victory was won by this small dependent troop who watched as God confused the enemy.

A classic example of this view of power is David's confrontation with Goliath. Is the point of the victory that Israel was mightier than Philistia? Obviously not. David's willingness to serve his people at the risk of his own life and his dependence on God completely reversed the expected outcome. David was victorious not because he had a great aim, but because of his dependence and service.

In II Kings 5 we see a drama of these conflicting views of power played out. Naaman was a great Syrian (Aram) warrior who had contracted leprosy. A servant girl instructed Naaman that there was a prophet in Israel who might be able to help him. To go to an Israelite prophet for help would be humiliating. Syria (Aram) was more powerful than Israel; to have to turn to the weaker nation would cast doubt both on the power of Syria and its deities. Yet Naaman was desperate. Having convinced his king that he should seek out this cure, Naaman left for Israel bearing the most splendid gifts and a letter of recommendation from his king. As he arrived in Samaria the intrigue of power develops.

The king of Israel was not a godly king and was himself caught with a bad view of power. The irony of power is that once you have a mistaken view, it influences most of your decisions. C. Wright Mills referred to this as "Crackpot Realism."[10] Mills says that people make power decisions based on what they perceive to be real circumstances. However, if their assumptions of what is real are mistaken, their decisions can seem realistic and yet be "crackpot." An example Mills uses is the assumption that war and not peace is the real state of affairs. To make decisions on that assumption as opposed to the assumption that peace is the natural state of affairs would have obvious consequences. The king of Israel's view of power becomes evident in this story.

Naaman, humble and desperate, came to the king of Israel with his letter of recommendation from his king. The letter asked the king of Israel to heal him of his leprosy. The irony is that Israel's king, so steeped in a bad view of power, could not recognize this humble, desperate man for what he is. Instead, he suspected international intrigue. He knew that there was no way he could heal Naaman. What he suspected was that the king of Syria knew he could not heal Naaman and that when he sent Naaman back uncured, it would provide excuse for an attack. Therefore, the king tore his robes and began to mourn his fate. But there was no intrigue; Naaman just wanted to be cured. The king looked like an utter fool.

One person, however, who did understand power in a biblical context, stepped in. Elisha the prophet, hearing of the king's distress, asked that Naaman be sent to him. The king of Israel's view of power was exposed and Naaman moved on.

Arriving at Elisha's house, with the regal splendor of horses, chariots, servants and treasures, Naaman was jolted. His assumption was that the prophet would wave his hands over him and shout a great incantation to heal him. Instead, Elisha did not even come out to see him, but sent word that he should go take a bath. Enraged, Naaman prepared to leave. Here we have a second view of power critiqued. We see that Naaman's humility was really due to his desperation. He would do anything to be cured. But the prophet's treatment of him rubbed his face in the dirt. No self-respecting warrior could take this kind of treatment; it would be better to die a slow death. Already embarrassed just by being in Israel, Naaman felt insulted. When he was told to take a dip in the murky Jordan river, Naaman was sure that the prophet wanted to humiliate him.

Naaman still thought that power resided in his dominant country, or in his strength or prestige as a famous warrior. But now that view of power was also undercut. The only one with real power in the story is Elisha. The irony is that by most views he seemed powerless. He was totally dependent on God for his power, and then he used that power to serve Naaman and others.

Naaman's servants convinced him to try the prophet's cure. Suspending his false view of power temporarily, he agreed. He followed the prophet's instructions and was cured. The cure is the final evidence of where true power resides. In acknowledgement of this, Naaman says, "Now I know that there is no God in all the world except in Israel."

The beauty of Naaman's confrontation with the prophet's godly power is that this time power did not dominate, coerce or confine him. He was not crushed by the prophet's power, but freed. True power served this diseased pagan and became a vehicle for grace. The prophet did not feel he had to show Naaman who was really the most powerful, but placed his certainty in the assurance that God would bring justice.

Power in the Bible is derived. It is lodged in the creator God who dispenses it as He pleases. The Old Testament witnesses to the constant problem of trying to locate power in the nation, the army, or the king. The people with real power end up being those who are able to connect to God's power. The major vehicle for obtaining that power is acknowledging dependence and demonstrating a willingness to serve others and the creation.

In the history of Israel there developed two strands of thought concerning the nature of the Messiah. The first was that the Messiah would be the great king in the Davidic line who would come to rule His people. The second was that the one in the line of David would come as a Suffering Servant. His would be a life of thankless pain and suffering. So divergent were these themes that they seemed to develop separately. So different did these two views seem that the Qumran community (a Jewish sect at the time of Jesus, which left the Dead Sea Scrolls) expected two different messiahs. As perplexing as it is to reconcile these two divergent views of the Messiah, it has been the church's confession throughout the ages that in Jesus those two roles came together. We confess that the Suffering Servant who dies becomes the conquering King in the line of David. Our attempts at reconciling the two tend to see Jesus as king at one time and servant at another.

However, a great deal of the problem is resolved if we put the dilemma in the context of the biblical understanding of power. The problem with reconciling the mighty king with the suffering servant is that we associate a king with the kind of power being critiqued. When we have thought about Christ as King we have assumed His ability to dominate. If we recover the biblical notion of power, the apparent contradiction of the roles is resolved. If power, as God ordained it, was to be dependence and service, what could be more biblically consistent than that the key possessor of power, the King, be the ultimate example of service? True power is gained in abiding by the structure God ordained for bestowing it. Christ's unspeakable power as the cosmic king was not the result of a cosmic weightlifting program or a cosmic arms build-up. Christ's power flowed directly from His qualities of dependence and service. How can we possibly affirm that this is so?

First, Christ's impact on history, equaled by no other person, was accomplished by His consistent refusal to use coercive forms of power. He clearly refused such power in the temptation and in the crucifixion, and His entire ministry was a demonstration of power residing in service. When John the Baptist was imprisoned and sent word asking if Jesus really was the Messiah, he was answered indirectly. Instead of pointing to might or ability to dominate, Jesus pointed to the service He had rendered as evidence of the inauguration of the Kingdom. He verifies His ministry and Messiahship by His service.

And second, in Philippians 2, Paul clearly links the service and dependence of Christ with His kingly power. Paul writes:

> Your attitude should be the same as that of Christ Jesus: Who, being in very nature God, did not consider equality with God something to be grasped, but made himself nothing, taking the very nature of a servant, being made in human likeness.
> And being found in appearance as a man, he humbled himself and became obedient to death—even death on a cross!
> Therefore God exalted him to the highest place and gave him the name that is above every name, that at the name of Jesus every knee should bow, in heaven and on earth and under the earth (Phil. 2:5-10 NIV).

Christ took upon Himself the form of a *servant*, and showing utter dependence upon God, humbled Himself and became obedient to the point of death. Not only does He exhibit service and dependence, but Paul says that because of those qualities, *therefore* God highly exalted Him.

The fact that Christ's lordship, His power, is derived from the qualities of dependence and service, usually seen as "weak" character traits, shatters our understanding of power. Who then has power? Is it those with mighty weapons? or great armies? or vast wealth? or public opinion on their side? Paul answers that question quite clearly in I Cor. 1:26-30 when he describes power-brokers in the Kingdom of God.

> Brothers, think of what you were when you were called. Not many of you were wise by human standards; not many were influential; not many were of noble birth. But God chose the foolish things of the world to shame the wise; God chose the weak things of the world to shame the strong. He chose the lowly things of the world and the despised things—and the things that are not—to nullify the things that are, so that no one may boast before him. It is because of him that you are in Christ Jesus, who has become for us wisdom from God—that is, our righteousness, holiness and redemption (I Cor. 1:26-30 NIV).

Paul could not be clearer about the proper perspective in which to see power when he says, "God chose what was weak in the world to shame the strong." But not only that, he takes the symbol which seems the essence of weakness and defeat, the cross, but which is really the essence of service, and calls it the *power* of God. "For the message of the cross is foolishness to those who are perishing, but to those who are being saved it is the power of God."

The implications of reversing our views of power are stirring. Kingdom power can never be lodged in military, political or economic dominance. If a nation, a people, a church or a person is to have power, that power must be characterized by dependence and service. Power in the kingdom demands that the strong live for the weak and serve the weak. They take up the cause of the weak against the powers that blindly oppress them.[11]

Does a nation become powerful by massing nuclear weapons or by feeding the starving millions? Does a people become powerful by maintaining the segregation of apartheid or by giving all people equal opportunity? Does a church become powerful by building a large edifice and increasing its budget or by preaching the good news to poor people? Is a person's strength measured in how many people "answer" to him or her or by how many people he or she serves? The power of Christ's Kingdom is very different. It will cause us to re-evaluate most of our relationships.

Of all the doubts that might arise about such a different notion of power, the most troubling is that everyone won't play by the same rules. What if I start serving people who use me, or dominate me, or who get ahead at my expense? People could seize this opportunity to invade, injure and destroy. But even as such objections are raised we realize that this is exactly what it cost Christ. Servanthood and dependence leave one weaponless. But history teaches us that when people have seized upon such opportunities against the defenseless, their dominance was temporary. Whether Ceasar, Napoleon, Hitler or Amin, the misuse of power eventually crumbles. False power alienates those whom it dominates. As those who are oppressed strive for freedom, false power has to become more and more repressive. Finally, the repression is too bitter and the false power crumbles. It is inevitable—whether communism, socialism, capitalism, or facism—if a system dominates people by false power it will eventually crumble. This can be confidently believed not just because of the witness of history, but because history itself is a testimony to the justice which God has built into the structure of His universe. This justice guarantees that false power is doomed to eventual failure.

A biblical perspective on power is very exciting. For power, one doesn't need wealth, position or strength. One merely needs to depend on God and serve others. True power is available for all of God's people. The places and positions we've normally viewed as domains of power are in many ways powerless.

This is the power that can energize the task of being a Christian student. It is this power which a student has available as he or she becomes immersed in one of the academic fields. Such a student must learn how to *depend* on God as the source of all knowledge. Such a student must have as his or her motive the desire to *serve* others by discovering the truth lodged in a particular discipline. Such service honors both the Creator and the creation.

The challenge to the Christian who is a student is to utilize the awesome power of God in your studies. Realize the pervasive corruption sin has brought to the task of being a student. Then pray, study and struggle to see the redemption of Christ realized in academics; anticipate the joy and fulfilment that accompanies the obedient response of a child of God; and recover the Godly task of being a Christian student in the colleges and universities of our world.